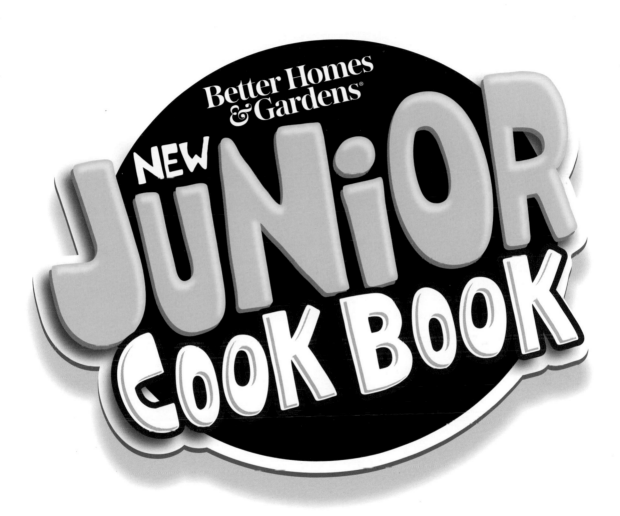

Better Homes & Gardens®

NEW JUNIOR COOK BOOK

Houghton Mifflin Harcourt
Boston · New York · 2018

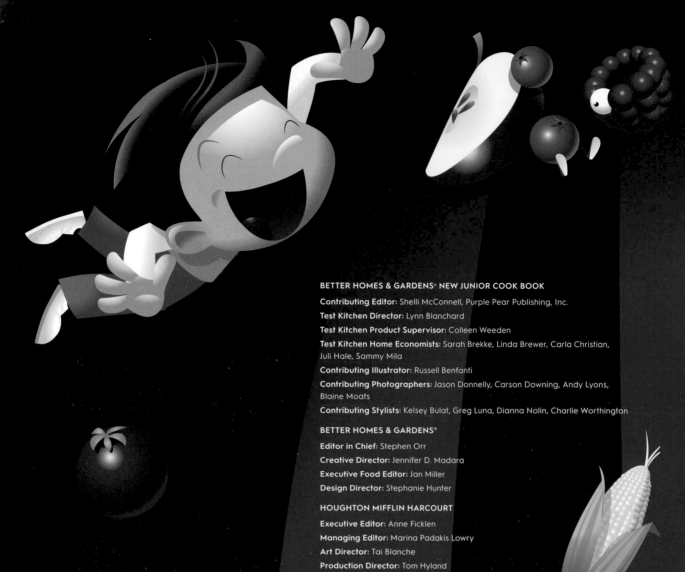

BETTER HOMES & GARDENS® NEW JUNIOR COOK BOOK

Contributing Editor: Shelli McConnell, Purple Pear Publishing, Inc.
Test Kitchen Director: Lynn Blanchard
Test Kitchen Product Supervisor: Colleen Weeden
Test Kitchen Home Economists: Sarah Brekke, Linda Brewer, Carla Christian, Juli Hale, Sammy Mila
Contributing Illustrator: Russell Benfanti
Contributing Photographers: Jason Donnelly, Carson Downing, Andy Lyons, Blaine Moats
Contributing Stylists: Kelsey Bulat, Greg Luna, Dianna Nolin, Charlie Worthington

BETTER HOMES & GARDENS®

Editor in Chief: Stephen Orr
Creative Director: Jennifer D. Madara
Executive Food Editor: Jan Miller
Design Director: Stephanie Hunter

HOUGHTON MIFFLIN HARCOURT

Executive Editor: Anne Ficklen
Managing Editor: Marina Padakis Lowry
Art Director: Tai Blanche
Production Director: Tom Hyland

WATERBURY PUBLICATIONS, INC.

Design Director: Ken Carlson
Editorial Director: Lisa Kingsley
Associate Editor: Tricia Bergman
Associate Editor: Mary Jo Plutt
Associate Design Director: Doug Samuelson
Associate Design Director: Becky Lau Ekstrand
Production Assistant: Mindy Samuelson
Contributing Copy Editor and Proofreader: Gretchen Kauffman, Carrie Truesdell

For information about permission to reproduce selections from this book, write to trade.permissions@hmhco.com or to Permissions, Houghton Mifflin Harcourt Publishing Company, 3 Park Avenue, 18th Floor, New York, NY 10016.

hmhco.com

Library of Congress Cataloging-in-Publication Data is available.

ISBN 9781328497680
Book design by Waterbury Publications, Inc., Des Moines, Iowa.

Printed in China

SCP 10 9 8 7 6 5 4 3 2 1

Better Homes & Gardens. TEST KITCHEN

Our seal assures you that every recipe in *Better Homes & Gardens® New Junior Cook Book* has been tested in the Better Homes & Gardens® Test Kitchen. This means that each recipe is practical and reliable and meets our high standards of taste appeal. We guarantee your satisfaction with this book for as long as you own it.

CONTENTS

COOKING IS FUN!

Hey, Kids! Head to the kitchen and learn to cook yummy, good-for-you recipes to help you power through your busy days. Grab an adult and read through the next few pages to learn the important stuff for making meals. Then pick a recipe, get cooking, and have fun!

START HERE

Read the recipe from start to finish. Make sure you understand exactly what to do. If you don't, ask an adult for help.

CHECK THE INGREDIENTS
Be sure you have everything you need. If you don't, make a list and ask to go shopping.

If you have food allergies, read the ingredients carefully to make sure all the foods are safe for you to eat.

FOLLOW THE RECIPE STEP-BY-STEP
Finish each step in the recipe before starting the next.

When you are done, be sure to clean up. Wash and dry dirty dishes, or load them into the dishwasher. Wipe counters with hot, soapy water. Put everything away.

FOR THE ADULTS
Teaching kids to cook gives them practical life skills and involving them in the kitchen gets them to eat more healthfully. You are the best teacher to help kids find success in cooking and eating well. Read the next pages with them and decide which recipe steps they may safely complete alone and which require your help. Guide them and let them do more as they progress. Most of all, be patient and make it fun!

4

SAFE COOKING

GREAT COOKS ARE SAFE COOKS.

KITCHEN SAFETY

Avoid kitchen accidents with this checklist.

☐ Have an adult helper show you how to use all kitchen tools safely.

☐ Roll up sleeves, pull back hair, and remove any loose clothing that might get in the way.

☐ Always pick up knives and scissors by the handles. Never put them in a sink of water, where they are hard to see. Have your adult helper show you how to use them safely.

☐ Use hot pads to remove things from the oven, stove top, or microwave.

☐ Be careful of steam—it is hot and can burn you. It builds up under pan lids and foil-covered dishes. Carefully lift the edge of the cover that is farthest away from you to let the steam out.

☐ Keep electric appliances away from the sink and stove. Water and electricity don't mix, and you don't want a cord to melt on a hot burner. Never touch the plug with wet hands.

☐ Unplug any electric appliance as soon as you are done with it. Turn off the oven and stove burners right away, too.

☐ Clean as you go. Wipe up spills and messes to prevent slips and falls. Keep the counter clean.

FOOD SAFETY

Handle food properly so you don't get sick.

☐ Wash your hands before you start. Wash them again after handling raw meat, poultry, and fish.

☐ Wash all fruits and veggies in cool water.

☐ Use a clean cutting board. Use separate boards for meats and veggies.

☐ Never eat raw meat and eggs. And don't put cooked food on a plate that had raw food on it.

☐ Cook food until it's done. Every recipe tells you when your food is done.

☐ Thaw frozen foods in the refrigerator overnight. Don't thaw on the counter.

KNOW THE TOOLS

BEFORE YOU START COOKING, MAKE SURE YOU HAVE THE TOOLS YOU NEED FOR THE RECIPE YOU'RE MAKING. THIS LIST SHOWS THE TOOLS YOU'LL USE MOST OFTEN.

Cookie sheet

Instant-read thermometer

Colander

Baking dish

Hot pad/ oven mitt

Fine-mesh sieve

Muffin pan

Kitchen scissors

Pancake turner

Whisk

Liquid measuring cup

Dry measuring cups

Sharp knife

Measuring spoons

Shallow baking pan

Baking pan

Wooden spoon

Can opener

Serrated knife

Silicone spatula

Skillet

Wire cooling rack

Saucepan

Electric mixer

Griddle

Vegetable peeler

Tongs

Citrus juicer

Pizza cutter

Slotted spoon

7

MEASURE RIGHT

THE INGREDIENTS LIST SHOWS HOW MUCH OF EACH INGREDIENT YOU NEED. FOLLOW THESE TIPS TO LEARN HOW TO MEASURE CORRECTLY.

LIQUIDS

Use liquid measuring cups. These cups are made of glass or plastic with a spout for easy pouring. Liquid measuring cups have lines on them to show amounts.

Set the cup on the counter. Pour in some of the liquid. Stand so your eyes are level with the markings on the side of the cup. Add or subtract little by little until you get to the right amount.

DRY INGREDIENTS

Measuring cups for dry ingredients come in sets that stack together. Each cup is sized and marked for a different amount—usually 1 cup, ½ cup, ⅓ cup, and ¼ cup. Some even have ⅔ and ¾ cups. Use a spoon to scoop ingredients such as flour and sugar into the cup size called for. Slide the flat side of a table knife across the top to make it smooth and push off any extra.

Pour ingredients like shredded cheese, cereal, and chocolate chips into the cup until even with the top. Don't pile it.

Measuring spoons work the same as cups and are used for small amounts of liquids, too.

FRACTION FIX!

Don't have a ¾ cup measure? Use a ¼ cup measure three times OR use a ¼ cup + ½ cup. For ⅔ cup, use the ⅓ cup measure two times.

SPECIAL INGREDIENTS

BROWN SUGAR
Brown sugar needs to be measured differently than other sugars. Spoon brown sugar into a dry measuring cup and use the back of a spoon to pack it firmly into the cup; add more as needed until it is level with the top of the cup.

STICKS OF BUTTER
One stick equals ½ cup. For smaller amounts, look for measurement marks on the wrapper and use a table knife to cut the wrapped stick at the amount you need.

PEANUT BUTTER AND SHORTENING
Use a silicone spatula to pack peanut butter or shortening in a dry measuring cup, making sure it's completely full. Level off the top with the flat edge of the silicone spatula to remove any extra. Be sure to scrape everything out of the cup.

SAFETY SECRET!

Never measure ingredients over the bowl or pan you are putting them in. You don't want to accidentally spill too much in.

WHAT DOES IT MEAN?

LEARN THESE COMMON COOKING TERMS—YOU WILL SEE THEM OFTEN IN THIS BOOK.

BEAT You can use a fork, electric mixer, or spoon to beat ingredients together, which adds air and combines them. Beating is a stronger motion than stirring. Lightly beaten eggs are mixed with a fork until the yolks and whites are the same color.

SLICE Use a knife—with an adult's help—and a cutting board to cut an ingredient, like a banana or carrot, across into pieces that are the same thickness.

CHOP Use a knife and a cutting board. First slice food evenly, then cut slices into lots of small pieces about the size of a pea. Finely chopped foods are half that size or smaller.

GREASE AND COAT Put some shortening or butter on a small piece of paper towel and rub evenly onto the inside of a pan to coat. When using nonstick cooking spray, cover the inside of the pan with a light spray. Be sure to spray over the sink so the floor doesn't get slippery.

TURN OVER Slide the flat part of a pancake turner under a food, such as a pancake. Lift the food straight up, then quickly flip it over to the other side.

PEEL Remove skin from vegetables or fruits with a vegetable peeler (like carrots or potatoes) or with your hands (like bananas). The blade on a vegetable peeler is sharp, so peel away from yourself and keep your fingers out of the way.

BOIL VS. SIMMER Food boils when it is cooked in a pan on the stove top over high heat until lots of big bubbles form quickly. To simmer, food is brought to a boil, then the heat is turned to low and often the pan is covered with a lid. The food will continue to boil slowly with little bubbles.

GRATED VS. SHREDDED Grated cheese, usually Parmesan from a container, is in small crumbly pieces. Shredded cheese, often sold in a bag, is in short strips.

Beat 2 Eggs?

MAKE A GREAT PLATE

USE THIS EATING GUIDE SO YOU CAN BE HEALTHY, STRONG, AND FULL OF ENERGY. IT SHOWS THE FIVE IMPORTANT FOOD GROUPS. TRY TO EAT A RAINBOW EVERY DAY.

WHAT MAKES A GREAT PLATE?

Start with a 9-inch plate and fill it as shown in the picture *below*.

FRUITS AND VEGETABLES Fill half your plate with these. Be sure to choose lots of different colors. (See "Eat the Rainbow," *opposite*.)

GRAINS The most healthful are whole grains, such as brown rice, oatmeal, and whole wheat pasta. Popcorn counts, too!

PROTEIN Choose different protein foods every day, such as lean meats, chicken, eggs, beans, nuts, and peanut butter. Try to eat fish twice a week—it keeps your brain and heart healthy.

DAIRY Serve milk or yogurt on the side and enjoy cheese as a snack.

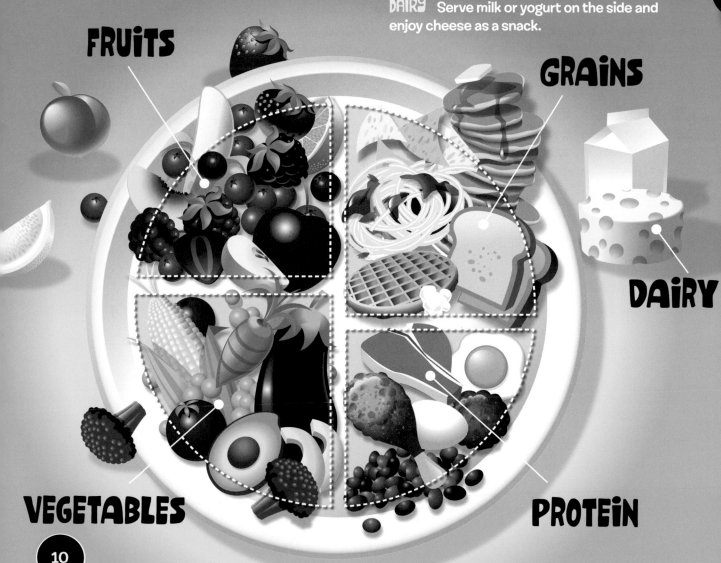

FRUITS

GRAINS

DAIRY

VEGETABLES

PROTEIN

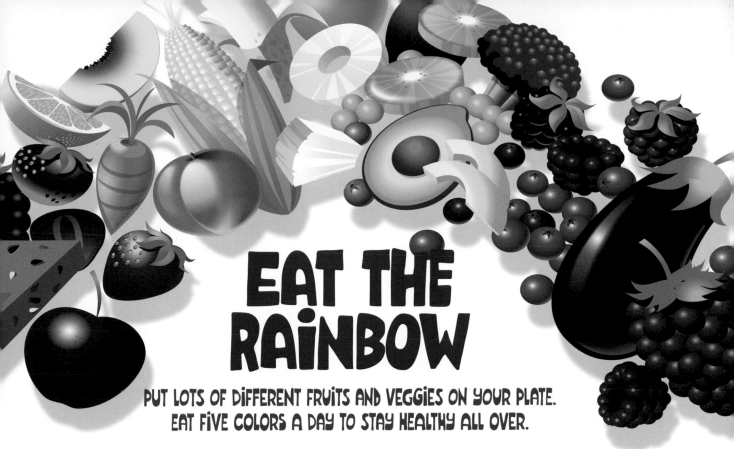

EAT THE RAINBOW

PUT LOTS OF DIFFERENT FRUITS AND VEGGIES ON YOUR PLATE.
EAT FIVE COLORS A DAY TO STAY HEALTHY ALL OVER.

RED (to keep your heart beating strong)

Red grapes
Red raspberries
Strawberries
Tomato
Watermelon
Red sweet pepper

ORANGE (to keep your eyes sharp)

Cantaloupe
Orange
Peach
Butternut squash
Carrot
Sweet potato

YELLOW (to keep you from getting sick)

Yellow apple
Banana
Pear
Pineapple
Corn
Yellow sweet pepper

GREEN (to keep your bones and teeth healthy)

Avocado
Kiwifruit
Green Beans
Broccoli
Peas
Spinach

BLUE AND PURPLE (to keep your brain smart)

Blackberries
Blueberries
Purple grapes
Plum
Eggplant
Purple cabbage

GOOD CHOICES

Some foods and drinks are okay to eat sometimes (candy, sports drinks, pizza, chips, cookies) but not every day, because they have lots of sugar or salt and may have unhealthy types of fat. When you can, choose apples instead of fries and water instead of soda pop. Pick snacks with protein, like cheese sticks, milk, and almonds, to keep you going.

SUPERPOWER BREAKFASTS

TIME TO REFUEL! USE THESE POWER-PACKED BREAKFASTS TO HELP YOU BLAST OUT OF THE HOUSE!

SECRET-IDENTITY PANCAKES

GIVE EACH PANCAKE ITS OWN DISGUISE WITH YOUR CHOICE OF SPRINKLE-ON.

MAKES 12 pancakes

INGREDIENTS

1	cup all-purpose flour
¾	cup whole wheat flour
2	Tbsp. sugar
2	tsp. baking powder
½	tsp. baking soda
¼	tsp. salt
1	egg
1½	cups buttermilk
3	Tbsp. vegetable oil
	Shortening
	SPRINKLE-ONS (optional)
	TOPPERS (optional)

TOOLS

Measuring cups and spoons, large bowl, medium bowl, fork, silicone spatula, griddle or large skillet, pancake turner, baking pan, hot pads

MAKE iT!

1 Turn on oven to 200°F. Put all-purpose and whole wheat flours, sugar, baking powder, baking soda, and salt in large bowl. Stir to mix.

2 Break egg into a medium bowl and beat with the fork. Add buttermilk and oil. Stir with the fork to mix.

3 Add egg mixture to flour mixture. Stir with the silicone spatula until flour mixture is wet. The batter should be a little lumpy, not smooth.

4 Grease an unheated griddle or large skillet with shortening. Put on burner. Turn burner to medium heat, and heat until a few drops of water sprinkled on the griddle or skillet dance across the surface.

5 For each pancake, pour about ¼ cup of the batter onto the hot griddle. (For dollar-size pancakes, use about 1 Tbsp. batter.) Spread batter if necessary. Sprinkle with one or more SPRINKLE-ONS. Cook 1 minute or until surface is bubbly and edges are slightly dry. Use the pancake turner to turn the pancakes over. Cook about 1 minute or until bottoms are golden brown.

6 Transfer pancakes to the baking pan. Put into oven to keep warm. Repeat until all batter is used. Use more shortening to grease griddle or skillet if needed. Turn off burner. Use hot pads to remove pancakes from oven. Turn off oven.

7 Put pancakes on plates. Top with one or more TOPPERS.

SPRINKLE-ONS Chopped fresh apple, peach, banana, or pear; fresh or frozen blueberries; miniature semisweet chocolate chips

TOPPERS Butter, desired syrup, chocolate-hazelnut spread, peanut butter, jelly

PER PANCAKE 122 cal., 4 g fat (1 g sat. fat), 17 mg chol., 220 mg sodium, 17 g carb., 1 g fiber, 4 g sugars, 4 g pro.

WAFFLES To make waffles, prepare batter as directed, except use 2 eggs and go up to ½ cup vegetable oil. Lightly grease waffle grids with shortening. Preheat waffle baker following manufacturer's directions. Add batter to the preheated waffle baker. Do not add SPRINKLE-ONS. Close lid quickly and do not open until done. Bake following manufacturer's directions. When done, carefully use a fork to lift waffle off grid. Repeat for remaining waffles.

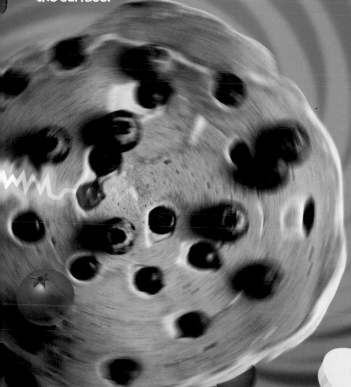

COOKING CLASS

If you don't have buttermilk, use regular milk, then go up to 1 Tbsp. baking powder and do not use the baking soda.

UPSIDE-DOWN SPIDERWEB CUPS

THESE EGG CUPS WILL MAKE YOUR SPIDER SENSE TINGLE.

MAKES 12 cups

INGREDIENTS

Shortening

12 frozen mini waffles, toasted

2 cups shredded cheddar cheese (8 oz.)

1 9- to 10-oz. package frozen cooked breakfast sausage links, thawed and chopped

6 eggs

3 Tbsp. milk

2 Tbsp. grated Parmesan cheese

½ tsp. black pepper

¼ tsp. salt

Maple syrup

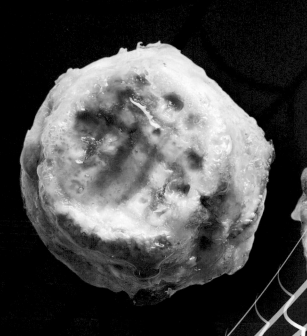

TOOLS

Measuring cups and spoons, cutting board, table knife, muffin pan with 2½-inch cups, medium bowl, fork, spoon, hot pads, wire rack

MAKE iT!

1 Turn on oven to 375°F. Grease the muffin cups with shortening. Put a mini waffle in each muffin cup. Divide 1 cup of the cheddar cheese evenly in the cups. Top evenly with sausage and the remaining 1 cup cheddar cheese.

2 Break the eggs into the medium bowl. Beat with the fork. Add the milk, Parmesan cheese, pepper, and salt. Stir with the fork to mix. Spoon mixture evenly into muffin cups.

3 Put muffin pan in oven. Bake 15 to 18 minutes or until set and golden brown. Turn off oven. Use hot pads to carefully remove muffin pan from oven. Put pan on a wire rack. Let cool 5 to 10 minutes.

4 Use the table knife to loosen spiderweb cups from muffin cups. Carefully remove the spiderweb cups. Drizzle with maple syrup.

TO MAKE AHEAD Cool the baked cups completely. Put cups in a single layer in an airtight container and cover it. Keep in the refrigerator up to 5 days or freeze up to 3 months. To serve, microwave one egg cup at a time until heated (15 to 20 seconds if refrigerated or 30 seconds if frozen).

PER CUP 221 cal., 15 g fat (6 g sat. fat), 131 mg chol., 443 mg sodium, 9 g carb., 0 g fiber, 5 g sugars, 12 g pro.

COOKING CLASS

Read the nutrition labels when you buy the sausage links. Pick one with the lowest amount of fat and sodium.

SPACE MONKEY BARS

BANANA-FLAVOR GRANOLA MAKES THESE BREAKFAST BARS OUT OF THIS WORLD.

MAKES 24 bars

INGREDIENTS

- 2 cups regular rolled oats
  Nonstick cooking spray
- 3/4 cup crunchy peanut butter
- 1/2 cup honey
- 3 Tbsp. coconut oil
- 2 Tbsp. unsweetened cocoa powder
- 2 cups banana-nut granola
- 2 cups whole grain wheat and brown rice cereal flakes, such as Total
- 1/2 cup salted roasted pepitas

TOOLS

Measuring cups and spoons, two 13×9-inch baking pans, hot pads, wire rack, foil, 4- to 6-qt. pot, wooden spoon, waxed paper, full food cans, cutting board, sharp knife

MAKE it!

1 Turn on the oven to 350°F. Spread oats in one 13×9-inch baking pan. Put pan in oven. Bake 7 minutes. Use hot pads to remove pan from oven. Stir oats. Use hot pads to put pan back in oven. Bake 5 to 8 minutes or until oats are golden. Turn oven off. Use hot pads to remove pan from oven. Put on a wire rack. Let oats cool.

2 Tear off a piece of foil that is about 20 inches long. Turn the second 13×9-inch baking pan over. Lay foil on the bottom of the pan and press it around the corners. Carefully lift foil off pan and turn pan over. Place the shaped foil into pan and press it to fit into the corners with extra hanging over the ends of pan. Coat foil with cooking spray.

3 Put the peanut butter, honey, coconut oil, and cocoa powder in the 4- to 6-qt. pot. Put pot on burner. Turn burner to medium heat. Cook and stir with the wooden spoon until melted and nearly smooth. Turn off burner. Use hot pads to remove pot from burner.

4 Put the oats, granola, cereal, and pepitas into the pot. Stir to mix well. Spoon mixture into the foil-lined pan. Using the wooden spoon, press the mixture firmly into the pan.

5 Put a piece of waxed paper over bars. Set the other pan inside and fill it with full food cans to weight mixture down. Put in the refrigerator 1 to 2 hours or until bars are firm enough to cut. Remove cans and pan. Using the foil, lift uncut bars from pan. Place on a cutting board. Remove foil. Use the knife to cut into 24 bars.

TO STORE Layer bars between sheets of waxed paper in an airtight container and cover with lid. Keep in the refrigerator up to 1 week or freeze up to 3 months.

PER BAR 195 cal., 11 g fat (3 g sat. fat), 0 mg chol., 74 mg sodium, 22 g carb., 3 g fiber, 9 g sugars, 6 g pro.

BODY BUILDER

Pepitas (the green kernels from a certain kind of pumpkin) are crunchy and delicious. They give you energy and contain the right kinds of fats to keep your brain sharp instead of spacey.

POWER-UP BREAKFAST COOKIES

GET ENERGIZED WITH THESE POWERHOUSE COOKIES WHEN YOU ARE CHARGING OUT THE DOOR.

MAKES 12 cookies

INGREDIENTS

- ½ cup mashed banana (1 large)
- ½ cup chunky peanut butter or almond butter
- ½ cup honey
- 2 Tbsp. fat-free milk or almond milk
- 1 tsp. vanilla
- 1 cup regular or quick-cooking rolled oats
- ½ cup whole wheat flour
- 2 tsp. ground cinnamon
- ¼ tsp. baking soda
- 1 cup dried cranberries, cherries, apples, or raisins

TOOLS

Measuring cups and spoons, 2 cookie sheets, parchment paper, large bowl, small bowl, wooden spoon, table knife, hot pads, pancake turner, wire rack

MAKE IT!

1 Turn on oven to 350°F. Line two cookie sheets with parchment paper. Put banana, peanut butter, honey, milk, and vanilla in the large bowl. Stir with the wooden spoon until mixed. Put oats, flour, cinnamon, and baking soda in the small bowl. Add oat mixture to banana mixture and stir until combined. Stir in dried cranberries.

2 Using a ¼-cup measure, scoop a cupful of dough and drop in a mound on a prepared cookie sheet. Scoop additional mounds onto cookie sheets, leaving 3 inches between dough mounds. Dip the table knife in water and use it to flatten and spread the mounds to 2¾-inch rounds (about ½ inch thick).

3 Put cookie sheets in oven. Bake 14 to 16 minutes or until cookies are browned. Turn off oven. Use hot pads to remove cookie sheets from oven. Use the pancake turner to transfer cookies to the wire rack to cool.

TO STORE Layer cookies between sheets of waxed paper in an airtight container and cover with lid. Store in the refrigerator up to 3 days or freeze up to 1 month.

PER COOKIE 193 cal., 6 g fat (1 g sat. fat), 0 mg chol., 80 mg sodium, 34 g carb., 3 g fiber, 21 g sugars, 4 g pro.

COOKING CLASS
Between scoops, coat the ¼-cup measure with nonstick cooking spray so it's easy to drop the dough.

UP & AWAY OATMEAL

FLY THROUGH BREAKFAST AND INTO YOUR DAY WITH THIS EASY MAKE-AHEAD OATMEAL.

MAKES 1 serving

INGREDIENTS

- ½ cup unsweetened almond milk
- ½ cup uncooked rolled oats
- 2 tsp. honey or pure maple syrup
- 2 Tbsp. fresh raspberries, blueberries, sliced strawberries, or chopped peaches
- 1 Tbsp. chopped toasted almonds

MAKE IT!

1 Put the almond milk, oats, and honey or maple syrup in a half-pint jar. Stir to mix well. Cover with the lid. Put in the refrigerator overnight.

2 When ready to eat, remove lid from jar. Stir the oats mixture. Top with fruit and almonds.

PER SERVING 263 cal., 8 g fat (1 g sat. fat), 0 mg chol., 91 mg sodium, 43 g carb., 6 g fiber, 14 g sugars, 7 g pro.

BODY BUILDER

Too much sugar in foods can keep you stuck on the ground. Instead, use natural sugars, like honey and maple syrup, whenever you can.

KA-POW BREAKFAST PUDDING

START YOUR DAY WITH A CREAMY, FRUITY PUNCH!

MAKES 6 servings

INGREDIENTS

- 1 14-oz. can unsweetened light coconut milk
- 1 cup plain fat-free Greek yogurt
- ¼ cup chia seeds
- 2 Tbsp. pure maple syrup
- ½ tsp. vanilla
- 2 cups chopped fresh fruit or berries, such as pineapple, strawberries, blueberries, mango, peach, and/or raspberries
- 6 tsp. unsweetened shredded coconut, toasted

MAKE IT!

1. Put the coconut milk, yogurt, chia seeds, maple syrup, and vanilla in a medium bowl. Stir to mix well. Spoon mixture into four serving bowls. Cover with foil. Put in the refrigerator overnight.

2. When ready to eat, uncover bowls. Spoon fruit and coconut over pudding in bowls.

PER SERVING 161 cal., 8 g fat (4 g sat. fat), 0 mg chol., 30 mg sodium, 18 g carb., 4 g fiber, 12 g sugars, 7 g pro.

BODY BUILDER

Chia seeds are tiny but mighty—they have protein to build muscles and calcium for stronger bones. When stirred into something wet like yogurt, the seeds get bigger with a jellylike coating on them to help fill you up.

23

QUICK-AS-A-FLASH
BACON & EGG CUP

IT ONLY TAKES 10 MINUTES TO MAKE THIS PROTEIN-PACKED CUP.

MAKES 1 serving

INGREDIENTS

Nonstick cooking spray
1 rich round cracker
1 egg
1 slice packaged ready-to-serve cooked bacon
1 Tbsp. shredded reduced-fat mild cheddar cheese

TOOLS

Measuring spoon, 4- to 6-oz. ramekin or custard cup, fork, kitchen scissors, waxed paper, hot pads, plate

MAKE IT!

1 Coat the microwave-safe 4- to 6-oz. ramekin or custard cup with cooking spray. Crumble the cracker into the bottom of the cup. Break the egg into the cup. Poke the yolk with the fork and stir it slightly. Snip the bacon into pieces with the kitchen scissors. Sprinkle bacon over the egg. Or curl the whole bacon strip to fit in cup and wrap around yolk.

2 Place cup in the microwave; cover with the waxed paper. Microwave 20 to 30 seconds or until egg is just cooked. Let stand 1 minute. Use hot pads to remove from microwave and put cup on the plate. Uncover and sprinkle with cheese. Serve in the cup.

PER SERVING 123 cal., 8 g fat (3 g sat. fat), 193 mg chol., 190 mg sodium, 3 g carb., 0 g fiber, 1 g sugars, 9 g pro.

COOKING CLASS

Charge up your cup! Use chopped ham or mini pepperoni instead of bacon. Try a different kind of cheese like mozzarella or Co-Jack. Top the cooked egg with pizza sauce or salsa.

EGGS-RAY SCRAMBLE

MAKES 4 servings

START

1

Break 8 EGGS into a medium bowl. Beat with a fork. Add ½ cup MILK. Stir to mix.

USE YOUR SUPERSIGHT TO PICK OUT THE BEST STUFF FOR THESE SCRAMBLED EGGS.

Ham

Crisp-cooked bacon

PICK

Sweet peppers

Spinach

Pepperoni

2

Choose one or more VEGETABLES to make 2 cups total.

Peas

Cooked sausage

PICK

3

Choose one or more MEATS to make ½ to 1 cup total.

Broccoli

Canned beans

26

FINISH

Spoon eggs onto plates. Sprinkle with TOPPERS.

6

PICK

Cheese

Avocado

Salsa

Pizza sauce

4

Put 2 Tbsp. BUTTER in a large skillet. Put on burner. Turn burner to medium-high heat. Add vegetables to skillet. Cook and stir just until vegetables are tender. Turn burner to medium heat. Add egg mixture and meats.

5

Let cook, without stirring, until mixture starts to set on bottom. With a silicone spatula, lift and turn the egg mixture 2 to 3 minutes or until it is cooked but still moist. Turn off burner. Use hot pads to remove skillet from burner.

ICE MASTER SMOOTHIES

THIS FRESH AND FROSTY SIPPER WILL GIVE YOU A BRISK START.

MAKES 2 servings

INGREDIENTS

- 1 5.3- to 6-oz. carton orange or lime Greek yogurt
- ½ cup orange juice or orange juice blend
- 2 Tbsp. honey or pure maple syrup
- ¼ tsp. vanilla
- 2 seedless clementines, peeled
- 2 cups fresh baby spinach
- 1 cup small ice cubes or crushed ice

BODY BUILDER

Spinach is super high in vitamin K, which builds strong bones. All that power and you can't even taste it!

TOOLS

Measuring cups and spoons, blender, 2 tall glasses

MAKE iT!

1 Put all ingredients in the blender in the order listed. Cover blender with lid. Blend on high speed 2 to 3 minutes or until smooth. Pour into glasses.

RED 209 cal., 1 g fat (1 g sat. fat), 4 mg chol., 64 mg sodium, 48 g carb., 2 g fiber, 43 g sugars, 5 g pro.

PEANUT BUTTER-BANANA Use vanilla yogurt instead of orange yogurt, milk instead of orange juice, and a small ripe banana instead of clementines. Add 2 Tbsp. peanut butter. Don't use spinach.

PER SERVING 294 cal., 11 g fat (3 g sat. fat), 9 mg chol., 155 mg sodium, 44 g carb., 2 g fiber, 34 g sugars, 10 g pro.

BERRY Use strawberry yogurt instead of orange yogurt, 1 cup halved fresh strawberries or fresh raspberries instead of clementines, and ½ cup chopped red sweet pepper instead of spinach.

202 cal., 1 g fat (1 g sat. fat), 4 mg chol., 44 mg sodium, 46 g carb., 2 g fiber, 42 g sugars, 4 g pro.

Use peach yogurt instead of orange yogurt and 1 cup frozen sliced peaches or chopped mangoes instead of clementines. Don't use spinach.

201 cal., 1 g fat (1 g sat. fat), 4 mg chol., 41 mg sodium, 46 g carb., 1 g fiber, 43 g sugars, 4 g pro.

FRENCH TOAST SABERS
WITH JAM DIPPING SAUCE

FIGHT YOUR WAY THROUGH A TOUGH MORNING WITH THIS POWER-PACKED BREAKFAST.

MAKES 6 servings

INGREDIENTS

Nonstick cooking spray

- $\frac{1}{4}$ cup ground flaxseeds
- 2 Tbsp. sugar
- $\frac{1}{2}$ tsp. ground cinnamon
- 3 eggs
- $\frac{1}{2}$ cup fat-free milk
- 1 Tbsp. sugar
- 1 tsp. vanilla
- 8 oz. hearty whole wheat bread
- $\frac{3}{4}$ cup strawberry, raspberry, or apricot spreadable fruit

Measuring cups and spoons, large baking sheet, shallow dish, medium bowl, fork, cutting board, sharp knife, hot pads, wire rack, small bowls

MAKE IT!

1 Turn on the oven to 450°F. Coat the large baking sheet with cooking spray; set aside. Put ground flaxseeds, the 2 Tbsp. sugar, and the cinnamon in the shallow dish. Break eggs into the medium bowl and beat with the fork. Add milk, the 1 Tbsp. sugar, and vanilla. Beat with the fork until well mixed.

2 Cut bread into twelve 1-inch-thick strips. Dip a bread strip in egg mixture, then roll it in flaxseed mixture to coat. Put coated strip on the prepared baking sheet. Repeat with remaining strips, placing them ½ inch apart on the prepared baking sheet

3 Put baking sheet in oven. Bake 12 to 15 minutes or until strips are light brown and crisp. Turn off oven. Use hot pads to remove baking sheet from oven. Set baking sheet on the wire rack.

4 Divide spreadable fruit among small bowls. Serve with toast strips for dipping.

TO MAKE AHEAD Let baked toast strips cool completely. Put them in an airtight container and cover with lid. Freeze up to 1 month. To serve, place four frozen toast strips on a microwave-safe plate. Microwave about 30 seconds or until hot. Serve toast strips with spreadable fruit.

PER SERVING 282 cal., 6 g fat (1 g sat. fat), 93 mg chol., 194 mg sodium, 49 g carb., 5 g fiber, 28 g sugars, 8 g pro.

DID YOU KNOW?
Use ground flaxseeds so you get the most nutrition from them. You can't digest whole flaxseeds.

FEEL-THE-BEAT LUNCHES

TRY THESE HOT OR COLD LUNCH CHOICES TO KEEP YOU GROOVIN' ON.

BEBOP MAC & CHEESE

MAKES 6 servings

INGREDIENTS

- 1⅓ cups dried elbow macaroni
- 3 cups chopped fresh broccoli
- 1 Tbsp. butter
- ¼ cup finely chopped onion
- 4 tsp. all-purpose flour
- ⅛ tsp. black pepper
- 1¼ cups fat-free milk
- 1 cup shredded reduced-fat cheddar cheese (4 oz.)
- 5 slices American cheese, torn (about 4 oz.)

THIS MAC AND CHEESE HAS A JAZZIER BEAT THAN ANYTHING YOU CAN GET FROM A BOX!

TOOLS

Measuring cups and spoons, large saucepan, wooden spoon, colander, hot pads, medium saucepan

MAKE iT!

1 Fill the large saucepan three-fourths full with cool water. Put pan on burner. Turn burner to medium-high heat. When water starts to boil, carefully add the macaroni to pan; stir with the wooden spoon. Cook following package directions until noodles are tender, stirring every now and then. About 4 minutes before macaroni should be done, add broccoli. Put the colander in sink. Turn off burner. Using the hot pads, carefully pour noodles and broccoli into colander to drain. Return macaroni and broccoli to hot saucepan; cover and keep warm.

2 Meanwhile, for cheese sauce, put butter in the medium saucepan. Put pan on burner. Turn burner to medium heat. When butter is melted, add onion and cook until tender, stirring every now and then with the wooden spoon. Stir in flour and pepper. Gradually pour in the milk while stirring. Cook and stir until slightly thickened and bubbly. Gradually add cheddar cheese and American cheese, stirring until cheeses melt. Turn off burner.

3 Using the hot pads, carefully pour cheese sauce over cooked macaroni and broccoli. Stir to mix. Put pan on burner. Turn burner to low heat. Cook 2 to 3 minutes or until heated through, stirring often. Turn off burner. Using the hot pads, remove pan from burner. Let stand 10 minutes before serving.

PER SERVING 275 cal., 12 g fat (7 g sat. fat), 38 mg chol., 491 mg sodium, 28 g carb., 2 g fiber, 5 g sugars, 15 g pro.

BODY BUiLDER

Putting little green broccoli trees in mac and cheese not only adds color, the fiber in it fills you up. Broccoli is a superfood that keeps you healthy.

CHICKEN GUITAR-BATTLE QUESADILLAS

THESE SPICY QUESADILLAS WILL HAVE YOU ROCKING OUT.

TOOLS

Measuring cups and spoons, cutting board, sharp knife, small bowl, spoon, cutting board, large skillet, pancake turner, pizza cutter

MAKES 4 servings

INGREDIENTS

- 1⅓ cups shredded rotisserie chicken
- 1 to 2 Tbsp. hot wing sauce
- 4 7- to 8-inch whole wheat flour tortillas
  Nonstick cooking spray
- ½ cup shredded part-skim mozzarella cheese (2 oz.)
- 2 Tbsp. crumbled blue cheese or shredded cheddar cheese
- 8 medium carrots, cut into sticks
- 6 stalks celery, cut into sticks
- ¼ cup light blue cheese or ranch salad dressing

1. Put the shredded chicken and hot wing sauce in the small bowl. Stir to mix.

2. Coat one side of each tortilla with cooking spray. Put tortillas, coated sides down, on the cutting board. Top half of each tortilla with mozzarella cheese, blue cheese, and shredded chicken. Fold tortillas in half, pressing gently.

3. Put two quesadillas in the large skillet. Put on burner. Turn burner to medium heat.

Cook quesadillas 2 minutes or until bottoms are golden. Using the pancake turner, carefully turn quesadillas over. Cook 2 to 3 minutes more or until cheeses are melted. Turn off burner. Remove quesadillas from skillet and put on the cutting board. Repeat with remaining two quesadillas.

4. Using the pizza cutter, cut quesadillas into wedges. Serve with carrots, celery, and salad dressing for dipping.

379 cal., 12 g fat (4 g sat. fat), 63 mg chol., 867 mg sodium, 40 g carb., 6 g fiber, 11 g sugars, 28 g pro.

COOKING CLASS
By changing the sauce, you can change the whole flavor of a recipe. Go sweet instead of spicy by using your favorite barbecue sauce instead of hot wing sauce. Or go extra cheesy and use Alfredo sauce.

PERFECT-PITCH GRILLED CHEESE ♪

MAKES 1 serving

HIT A NEW NOTE EVERY TIME YOU MAKE A GRILLED CHEESE SANDWICH.

START

1
Use a table knife to spread 1 Tbsp. BUTTER on one side of 2 BREAD slices.

PICK
Wheat bread
White bread
Cinnamon-raisin bread

Co-Jack
Muenster

PICK

2
Place one bread slice, spread side down, in a cold nonstick skillet. Top with one slice of CHEESE.

Provolone
American

3
If you wish, add one or two FILLINGS. Then add another slice of cheese and add the last bread slice, spread side up.

PICK
Apple slices
Pepperoni
Crisp-cooked bacon
Salami
Ham
Turkey
Fresh spinach

MAKE IT A QUESADILLA
Use a 7- to 8-inch flour tortilla. Layer CHEESE and FILLING on half of the tortilla, tearing cheese to fit, then fold tortilla in half over top. Cook as directed, buttering the outside of folded tortilla.

FINISH

Fruit jelly

PICK

Ranch dressing

Ketchup

⑤ If you like, eat sandwich with a DIP of your choice.

Pizza sauce

Mustard

Basil pesto

④ Put skillet on burner. Turn burner to medium heat. Cook until sandwich bottom is golden brown.

Use a pancake turner to carefully turn the sandwich over. Cook until bottom is golden and cheese is melted.

MY-OWN-BEAT SUB SLIDERS

HONEY MUSTARD AND TANGY CHEDDAR CHEESE TURN UP THE VOLUME IN THESE MINI SANDWICHES.

MAKES 1 sandwich

INGREDIENTS

- 1 Hawaiian sweet roll or slider-size pretzel roll
- ½ tsp. honey mustard
- ½ tsp. light mayonnaise
- 1 oz. thinly sliced deli ham or turkey breast
- 1 slice white cheddar or provolone cheese
- Fresh spinach (optional)

COOKING CLASS

On a chilly day, a hot sandwich tastes good. Just put your sandwich on a microwave-safe plate and microwave about 15 seconds or until cheese is melted.

TOOLS

Measuring spoon, cutting board, serrated knife, table knife

MAKE iT!

1. Using the serrated knife, cut roll in half. Using the table knife, spread one cut side of roll with honey mustard and one cut side with mayonnaise. Top the bottom half of the roll with ham, cheese, and, if you like, a few spinach leaves. Add the top of the roll.

PER SANDWICH 236 cal., 12 g fat (6 g sat. fat), 53 mg chol., 558 mg sodium, 20 g carb., 1 g fiber, 9 g sugars, 14 g pro.

41

RAPPIN' BBQ WRAPPERS

BUST A RHYME WITH THIS CRUNCHY, SAUCY WRAP.

MAKES 1 wrap

INGREDIENTS

- 4 oz. cooked roast beef or turkey, shredded or thinly sliced (¾ cup)
- 1 7- to 8-inch whole wheat or plain flour tortilla
- 2 Tbsp. barbecue sauce
- ⅓ to ½ cup packaged shredded coleslaw mix
- 2 to 3 Tbsp. shredded Monterey Jack cheese

1 Put the beef or turkey evenly on the tortilla. Drizzle barbecue sauce on the beef. Top with coleslaw and cheese. Roll up tortilla.

PER WRAP 307 cal., 12 g fat (5 g sat. fat), 51 mg chol., 534 mg sodium, 21 g carb., 10 g fiber, 5 g sugars, 25 g pro.

TOOLS

Measuring cups and spoons

COOKING CLASS

If you are making the wrap to eat later, have a piece of plastic wrap ready to go on the counter. Place the rolled tortilla on the plastic wrap, then tightly pull the plastic wrap around it to keep it together. Put the wrap in the refrigerator up to a day. To take it for lunch, place it in an insulated lunch box with an ice pack.

DRUM LINE SALAD CUPS

THESE SALAD CUPS WILL LAY DOWN A SOLID BEAT TO KEEP YOU MARCHING ALL DAY.

MAKES 4 servings

INGREDIENTS

- ¼ cup plain low-fat yogurt
- ¼ cup light ranch salad dressing
- 1½ cups coarsely chopped cooked chicken or turkey
- ½ cup coarsely chopped red and/or yellow sweet pepper
- ¼ cup shredded carrot
- ¼ cup chopped pecans or walnuts (optional)

BODY BUILDER

Sweet peppers have more vitamin C than oranges, which can help keep you from getting a cold. To see better at night, crunch some vitamin-A-loaded carrots.

TOOLS

Measuring cups, small bowl, spoon, medium bowl, 4 plastic cups, plastic wrap

MAKE IT!

1 Put yogurt and salad dressing in the small bowl; use the spoon to stir and mix well. Put chicken, sweet pepper, carrot, and, if you like, nuts in the medium bowl; stir to mix. Pour yogurt mixture over chicken mixture; stir to coat.

2 For individual lunches, divide chicken mixture among the plastic cups. Cover cups with plastic wrap. Put in the refrigerator up to 24 hours.

PER SERVING 148 cal., 7 g fat (2 g sat. fat), 48 mg chol., 172 mg sodium, 4 g carb., 1 g fiber, 3 g sugars, 16 g pro.

45

TUNA
HEAVY METAL MELTS

THESE TUNA MELTS WILL HAVE YOU SCREAMING FOR MORE.

MAKES 4 sandwiches

INGREDIENTS

- ½ of a medium avocado, seeded, peeled, and cut up
- 1⅓ cups packaged shredded broccoli (broccoli slaw mix)
- 3 Tbsp. bottled light ranch salad dressing
- 2 5-oz. cans chunk light tuna (water pack), drained and flaked
- ¼ cup chopped celery
- 2 to 3 Tbsp. thinly sliced green onion
- 2 Tbsp. light mayonnaise
- 1 Tbsp. Dijon-style mustard
- 1 Tbsp. lemon juice
- 4 slices whole wheat bread
- 4 ultrathin slices cheddar cheese,* cut into strips

TOOLS

Measuring cups and spoons, cutting board, sharp knife, baking sheet, small bowl, fork, can opener, medium bowl, spoon, hot pads, pancake turner

MAKE IT

1. Put an oven rack in the top third of the oven so the baking sheet is about 6 inches from the broiler. Turn on the broiler. Put the avocado in the small bowl and mash with the fork until spreadable. You can leave some chunks or mash it until it's smooth. Add broccoli slaw mix and salad dressing. Stir to mix.

2. Put the tuna, celery, green onion, mayonnaise, mustard, and lemon juice in the medium bowl. Using the spoon, stir to mix.

3. Put bread slices on the baking sheet. Carefully put pan under broiler on top of rack. Broil about 2 minutes or until bread is lightly toasted. Using the hot pads, remove pan from broiler. Use the pancake turner to turn bread over. Use hot pads to put pan back under broiler. Broil 2 minutes more or until bread is toasted on other side. Use hot pads to remove pan.

4. Spoon broccoli slaw mixture onto toasted bread slices. Top with tuna mixture and cheese strips.

5. Use hot pads to carefully place pan under broiler. Broil 2 to 3 minutes or until cheese is melted. Use hot pads to remove pan from oven.

TIP If you can't find the ultrathin slices of cheese, use reduced-fat sliced cheddar cheese.

PER SANDWICH 308 cal., 14 g fat (4 g sat. fat), 33 mg chol., 601 mg sodium, 29 g carb., 5 g fiber, 3 g sugars, 19 g pro.

HOEDOWN CHICKEN RANCH FLATBREADS

ROPE YOURSELF A PARTNER TO SHARE THESE MIGHTY GOOD FLATBREADS.

MAKES 4 servings

INGREDIENTS

- 2 rustic white or spicy Italian artisan pizza thin-crust flatbreads
- 3 Tbsp. light sour cream
- 3 Tbsp. light ranch salad dressing
- 1 cup shredded cooked chicken breast
- 1 cup shredded part-skim mozzarella cheese (4 oz.)
- 2 cups chopped romaine lettuce
- ½ cup quartered cherry tomatoes
- ¼ cup finely shredded Parmesan cheese
- 2 slices packaged ready-to-serve bacon, cut up

MAKE IT!

1. Preheat oven to 450°F. Cut pizza flatbreads in half crosswise using the pizza cutter. Place flatbreads on the large baking sheet. Carefully put baking sheet in oven. Bake 4 minutes. Using the hot pads, remove baking sheet from oven.

2. Put sour cream and dressing in the medium bowl. Stir to mix. Spread 3 Tbsp. of the mixture over flatbreads. Top with chicken and mozzarella. Bake 3 to 5 minutes more or until cheese is melted and crust is golden brown.

3. Meanwhile, add the lettuce to the remaining 2 Tbsp. sour cream-dressing mixture. Stir to coat. Top flatbreads with lettuce and sprinkle with tomatoes, Parmesan cheese, and bacon.

PER SERVING 276 cal., 13 g fat (6 g sat. fat), 58 mg chol., 554 mg sodium, 15 g carb., 2 g fiber, 3 g sugars, 24 g pro.

TOOLS

Measuring cups and spoons, cutting board, pizza cutter, large baking sheet, hot pads, medium bowl, spoon, table knife, sharp knife

TANGO TORTELLINI STEW

THIS SAUCY STEW WILL HAVE YOU DANCING THE TANGO.

INGREDIENTS

- 1 Tbsp. olive oil
- 1 8-oz. package sliced fresh mushrooms (3 cups)
- ½ cup chopped onion
- 2 14.5-oz. cans no-salt-added diced tomatoes, undrained
- 1 14.5-oz. can vegetable broth
- 1 8-oz. can no-salt-added tomato sauce
- ½ cup bottled salsa
- 2 tsp. dried Italian seasoning, crushed
- 1 9- to 10-oz. package refrigerated cheese-filled tortellini

  Shredded Italian-blend cheeses (optional)

TOOLS

Measuring cups and spoons, cutting board, sharp knife, can opener, 4- to 5-qt. pot, wooden spoon

MAKE IT!

1 Put oil in the 4- to 5-qt. pot. Put pot on burner. Turn burner to medium heat. When oil is hot, put mushrooms and onion in pot. Cook 5 to 8 minutes or until mushrooms are tender, stirring now and then with the wooden spoon.

2 Add tomatoes, vegetable broth, tomato sauce, salsa, and Italian seasoning to the pot. Stir to mix. Add tortellini. Turn burner up to medium-high heat. Bring soup to boiling. Turn burner down to medium-low heat. Cover pot with the lid and simmer about 10 minutes or until tortellini are tender, stirring now and then with the wooden spoon. Turn off burner.

3 If you like, top each serving with some cheese.

PER 1 CUP 141 cal., 3 g fat (1 g sat. fat), 11 mg chol., 431 mg sodium, 23 g carb., 4 g fiber, 7 g sugars, 6 g pro.

COOKING CLASS
Make this stew, or any recipe that calls for salsa, mild or spicy depending on the hotness of salsa you choose.

CHA-CHA SALAD TACOS

EAT A SALAD WITH YOUR HANDS AND YOU WON'T HAVE TO STOP DANCING.

INGREDIENTS

- 1 cup pinto beans, drained but not rinsed
- ½ cup frozen corn kernels, thawed
- ½ cup chopped zucchini
- ½ cup guacamole
- 4 6-inch flour tortillas
- ¼ cup salsa

TOOLS

Measuring cups and spoons, fine-mesh sieve, cutting board, sharp knife, medium bowl, spoon

MAKE IT!

1. Put the beans, corn, and zucchini in the medium bowl. Using the spoon, stir to mix.

2. Spread about 2 Tbsp. of the guacamole onto each tortilla. Top evenly with vegetable mixture and salsa. Fold each taco in half to serve.

TIP If you like, add any chopped leftover grilled meat, such as chicken, shrimp, beef steak, or pork chops.

PER TACO 235 cal., 8 g fat (2 g sat. fat), 0 mg chol., 671 mg sodium, 33 g carb., 7 g fiber, 3 g sugars, 8 g pro.

When you open the can of beans, you will see there is liquid in the can. Pour the beans into a fine-mesh sieve that is set in the sink or over a bowl so they can drain. Any liquid that is still clinging to the beans will help the vegetable mixture stick together.

HIGH-NOTE CHEESEBURGER SOUP

THIS BURGER-IN-A-BOWL WILL HAVE YOU SINGING FOR MORE.

MAKES 10 cups

INGREDIENTS

- 1 lb. extra-lean ground beef
- ½ cup chopped onion
- 2 Tbsp. butter
- 2 Tbsp. all-purpose flour
- 1¾ cups water
- 1 14.5-oz. can vegetable broth
- 1 cup milk
- 2 medium (6 oz. each) potatoes, coarsely chopped
- 12 slices American cheese, torn
- 1 14.5-oz. can no-salt-added diced tomatoes, drained
- 1 6-oz. can no-salt-added tomato paste
- ¼ cup ketchup
- 1 Tbsp. yellow mustard
- Dill pickles (optional)

TOOLS

Measuring cups and spoons, cutting board, sharp knife, can opener, 4- to 5-qt. pot, wooden spoon, whisk

MAKE iT!

1 Put beef and onion in the 4- to 5-qt. pot. Put on burner. Turn burner to medium-high heat. Cook until meat is browned, stirring with the wooden spoon and breaking up meat as it cooks.

2 Turn burner to medium heat. Add butter to pot. Melt butter. Sprinkle flour over beef mixture and stir to combine. Add the water, broth, and milk. Whisk to mix. Stir in potatoes. Turn burner up to medium-high heat. Bring to boiling, stirring occasionally. Turn burner down to medium-low heat. Cover pot. Simmer about 12 minutes or until potatoes are very tender, stirring occasionally. Using the back of the wooden spoon, lightly mash some of the potatoes into the soup.

3 Add the cheese. Cook and stir until cheese is melted and smooth. Add tomatoes, tomato paste, and ketchup. Stir to mix. Heat through. Turn off burner. Stir in mustard.

4 If you like, top each serving of soup with pickles.

PER 1 CUP 253 cal., 13 g fat (7 g sat. fat), 59 mg chol., 659 mg sodium, 17 g carb., 3 g fiber, 7 g sugars, 16 g pro.

COOKING CLASS

This soup makes a lot, but that's great. There will be leftovers, and this soup is even better the next day! Store extra soup in an airtight container. Reheat it in a saucepan over medium-low heat, stirring every now and then.

SPORTIN'-AROUND SUPPERS

SCORE BIG WITH A SATISFYING MEAL TO RUN OUT THE CLOCK WHEN IT'S TIME TO EAT.

HOLE-IN-ONE SPAGHETTI & MEATBALL PIES

HEAD TO THE CLUBHOUSE FOR THESE ACE-IN-THE-HOLE MINI PASTA PIES.

MAKES 6 servings

INGREDIENTS

Nonstick cooking spray

4 oz. whole grain or multigrain thin spaghetti (tip, *page 77*), broken in half

1 egg

⅓ cup grated Parmesan cheese

1 Tbsp. milk

1 12-oz. package (12) refrigerated cooked Italian-style turkey or chicken meatballs

½ of a 23.8-oz. jar (1¼ cups) light no-sugar-added tomato and basil pasta sauce

½ cup shredded reduced-fat Italian-blend cheeses

TOOLS

Measuring cups and spoons, muffin pan with twelve 2½-inch cups, large saucepan, wooden spoon, colander, hot pads, large bowl, fork, spoon, wire rack, table knife

MAKE IT!

1 Preheat oven to 350°F. Coat twelve 2½-inch muffin cups with cooking spray (tip, *page 71*). Fill the large saucepan three-fourths full with cool water. Put on burner. Turn burner to medium-high heat. When water starts to boil, carefully add the spaghetti; stir with the wooden spoon. Cook following package directions until noodles are tender, stirring every now and then. Put colander in sink. Turn off burner. Using the hot pads, carefully pour noodles into colander to drain.

2 Meanwhile, break egg into the large bowl. Lightly beat egg with the fork. Add Parmesan cheese and milk. Stir to mix. Add the cooked pasta. Stir to mix. Spoon the spaghetti mixture evenly into the prepared muffin cups. Use the back of the spoon to press the spaghetti onto bottoms and slightly up sides of cups. Add a meatball to each cup. Spoon sauce evenly over meatballs.

3 Carefully put pan in the oven. Bake 15 minutes. Use hot pads to remove pan from oven. Carefully sprinkle meatballs with Italian cheese. Use hot pads to put pan back in oven. Bake 2 minutes more or until cheese is melted. Turn off oven. Use hot pads to remove pan from oven. Put pan on a wire rack; cool in muffin cups 5 minutes. Use the table knife to remove pies from muffin cups. If you like, serve pies with additional warmed pasta sauce.

PER SERVING 283 cal., 11 g fat (4 g sat. fat), 83 mg chol., 719 mg sodium, 22 g carb., 3 g fiber, 4 g sugars, 21 g pro.

COOKING CLASS

Put it on the green with a crunchy salad. Fill a bowl with torn lettuce leaves, shredded carrot, and chopped red sweet pepper, then top it with your favorite salad dressing.

SURF'S-UP FISH FINGERS

THESE CRISPY BAKED FISH FINGERS WILL HAVE YOU CATCHING THE NEXT BIG WAVE!

INGREDIENTS

1½ lb. fresh or frozen cod or other whitefish fillets, about 1 inch thick

Nonstick cooking spray

½ cup all-purpose flour

5 tsp. ranch dry salad dressing mix

3 eggs

2 cups panko bread crumbs

2 Tbsp. butter, melted

1 tsp. dry mustard

½ tsp. black pepper

MAKE IT!

1 Thaw fish if frozen. Turn on oven to 450°F. Line the large baking sheet with foil. Coat foil with cooking spray. Rinse fish under cold water; pat dry with the paper towels. Use the sharp knife to cut fish into 3¾-inch strips.

2 In a shallow dish stir together the flour and dressing mix. Break the eggs into a separate shallow dish. Lightly beat eggs with the fork. In a third shallow dish combine the bread crumbs, butter, dry mustard, and pepper; stir to evenly coat crumbs.

3 Dip fish strips in flour mixture, then eggs, then bread crumb mixture to coat, turning and pressing to stick coating to fish. Place fish on the foil-lined baking sheet. Lightly coat tops of fish strips with cooking spray.

TOOLS

Measuring cups and spoons, large baking sheet, foil, paper towels, sharp knife, cutting board, 3 shallow dishes, fork, hot pads

TIDE'S-OUT TACOS

Use fish or chicken fingers to fill warm corn or flour tortillas. Add your favorite taco fillings, such as shredded cheese, chopped lettuce, avocado, and tomatoes.

4 Carefully put pan in oven. Bake about 10 minutes or until golden and fish flakes easily when tested with a fork. Turn off oven. Use hot pads to remove pan from oven. Serve fish with desired dipping sauce (*below* and *right*).

PER SERVING 256 cal., 7 g fat (3 g sat. fat), 151 mg chol., 356 mg sodium, 19 g carb., 1 g fiber, 1 g sugars, 26 g pro.

SURF'S-UP CHICKEN FINGERS
Prepare as directed, except substitute 1½ lb. chicken tenders for fish. Bake about 12 minutes or until chicken is no longer pink.

PER SERVING 299 cal., 9 g fat (4 g sat. fat), 185 mg chol., 346 mg sodium, 19 g carb., 1 g fiber, 1 g sugars, 31 g pro.

HANG-TEN HONEY MUSTARD SAUCE
Put ¼ cup light mayonnaise and 2 Tbsp. honey mustard in a bowl. Stir to mix.

PIPELINE PICKLE DIP
Put ¼ cup mayonnaise, ¼ cup plain low-fat Greek yogurt, 3 Tbsp. ketchup, 1 Tbsp. ranch dry salad dressing mix, and 1 Tbsp. dill pickle relish in a bowl. Stir to mix.

COWABUNGA RANCH DIP
Put ⅓ cup plain low-fat Greek yogurt and 2 tsp. ranch dry salad dressing mix in a bowl. Stir to mix.

HALF-PIPE NOODLES
WITH CHICKEN SAUSAGE

SHOW OFF YOUR BOARD TRICKS AFTER DOWNING THIS SWEET AND SASSY NOODLE BOWL.

MAKES 4 servings

INGREDIENTS

- ½ of an 8-oz. package (1 packet) dried brown rice noodles
- 1 20-oz. can pineapple chunks (juice pack)
- 1 tsp. cornstarch
- ½ tsp. ground ginger
- ¼ tsp. crushed red pepper
- 4 cooked chicken sausage links with spinach and garlic
  Nonstick cooking spray
- 1 6-oz. package fresh snow pea pods

TOOLS

Measuring cups and spoons, colander, hot pads, kitchen scissors, can opener, fine-mesh sieve, liquid measuring cup, whisk, sharp knife, cutting board, large nonstick skillet, wooden spoon

MAKE IT!

1 Prepare rice noodles following package directions. Put the colander in sink. Using hot pads, carefully pour rice noodles into colander to drain. Rinse with hot water from the faucet; drain again. If desired, use the kitchen scissors to snip noodles into shorter lengths.

2 Meanwhile, drain pineapple in a fine-mesh sieve over a liquid measuring cup. Measure ¾ cup of the juice and discard the rest. Add cornstarch, ginger, and crushed red pepper to the pineapple juice. Use a whisk to mix well. Use the sharp knife to cut each sausage into eight slices.

3 Lightly coat the inside of the large nonstick skillet with cooking spray. Add sausage slices and pea pods to skillet. Put skillet on burner. Turn burner to medium-high heat. Cook 4 to 5 minutes or until sausage is lightly browned and pea pods are bright green and a little tender, using the wooden spoon to stir now and then.

4 Turn burner to medium heat. Stir pineapple juice mixture and carefully add it to the skillet. Cook and stir constantly with the wooden spoon until thickened and bubbly. Cook and stir 2 minutes more. Stir in 1 cup of the pineapple chunks (save the remaining pineapple for another use). Turn off burner. Stir in rice noodles.

PER SERVING 253 cal., 4 g fat (1 g sat. fat), 50 mg chol., 523 mg sodium, 41 g carb., 2 g fiber, 13 g sugars, 16 g pro.

DID YOU KNOW?

Pineapple chunks are packed in cans with either juice or a thick syrup. The best for you is juice-pack pineapple, and it tastes good, too!

CLIMB-TO-THE-TOP MEAT SUNDAES

SCALE THIS MOUNTAIN OF POTATOES AND ITS PEAK OF BEEF SAUCE TO PLANT A CHERRY (TOMATO) ON TOP!

MAKES 4 servings

INGREDIENTS

Nonstick cooking spray

1 lb. lean beef stew meat

1 14.5-oz. can reduced-sodium beef broth

1 tsp. bottled minced garlic

¼ tsp. black pepper

¼ cup cold water

2 Tbsp. all-purpose flour

1 24-oz. package refrigerated mashed potatoes (2½ cups)

¼ cup shredded reduced-fat cheddar cheese

¼ cup sliced green onions (optional)

4 cherry tomatoes

TOOLS

Measuring cups and spoons, can opener, medium saucepan, wooden spoon, slotted spoon, pie plate, 2 forks, liquid measuring cup, small bowl, whisk, ice cream scoop, cutting board, sharp knife

MAKE IT!

1 Coat the medium saucepan with cooking spray. Put pan on burner. Turn burner to medium-high heat. Add half of the stew meat. Cook until meat is no longer pink, stirring with the wooden spoon now and then. Use the slotted spoon to carefully move cooked meat to the pie plate. Repeat with the remaining uncooked meat.

2 Return all meat to the pan. Carefully add broth, garlic, and pepper. Turn burner to high heat. Bring to boiling. Turn down heat to medium-low. Cover and cook about 1 hour or until you can put a fork in the meat and it falls apart. Turn off burner. Using the slotted spoon, move meat to the pie plate. Cool slightly. Use the two forks to pull meat apart into shreds.

3 Spoon 1 cup cooking liquid in pan into the liquid measuring cup; discard any remaining liquid in the pan. Return the 1 cup liquid to pan. In the small bowl combine the cold water and flour. Stir until smooth. Carefully stir flour mixture into cooking liquid in pan. Turn burner to medium heat. Cook and stir with the whisk until liquid is thickened and bubbly; cook and stir 1 minute more. Carefully return shredded meat to pan; stir to mix. Turn off burner.

4 Heat mashed potatoes following package directions. Use the ice cream scoop to put a mound of mashed potatoes into each bowl. Top with beef mixture, cheese, and, if desired, green onions. Top each "sundae" with a tomato.

PER SERVING 324 cal., 12 g fat (6 g sat. fat), 94 mg chol., 926 mg sodium, 24 g carb., 3 g fiber, 2 g sugars, 31 g pro.

BODY BUILDER

Lean beef has lots of protein to build strong muscles and get you to the top.

SWIM FINS TORTILLA SOUP

STAY IN THE HEALTHY-EATING LANE WITH THIS STRONG-STROKE SOUP.

MAKES 10 cups

INGREDIENTS

- 1 Tbsp. vegetable oil
- 1 cup chopped onion
- 1 tsp. ground cumin
- 1 32-oz. carton reduced-sodium chicken broth
- 2 14.5-oz. cans no-salt-added fire-roasted diced tomatoes, undrained
- 1½ cups coarsely shredded cooked chicken breast
- 1½ cups frozen whole kernel corn
- 2 4-oz. cans diced green chile peppers, undrained
- 2 cups coarsely crushed tortilla chips
  Snipped fresh cilantro (optional)
  Shredded Monterey Jack cheese (optional)

TOOLS

Measuring cups and spoons, sharp knife, cutting board, can opener, 4-qt. pot, wooden spoon

MAKE IT!

1 Put oil in the 4-qt. pot. Put pot on burner. Turn burner to medium heat. Add onion and cumin. Cook about 5 minutes or until onion is tender, stirring often with the wooden spoon. Carefully add chicken broth, tomatoes, chicken, corn, and chile peppers. Turn burner to high heat. Bring to boiling; turn heat to medium low. Cover and simmer 10 minutes. Turn off burner.

2 Serve soup in bowls. Divide crushed tortilla chips among bowls. If you wish, sprinkle with cilantro and cheese.

PER 1²/₃ CUPS 265 cal., 8 fat (1 g sat. fat), 30 mg chol., 562 mg sodium, 31 g carb., 3 g fiber, 7 g sugars, 18 g pro.

COOKING CLASS

To crush tortilla chips without making a mess, put them in a resealable plastic bag. Seal the bag, then roll over the chips with a can of food or a rolling pin to crush.

PUMP-iT-UP VEGGiE SOUP

BUILD YOUR MUSCLES BY LIFTING SPOONFULS OF THIS NUTRITION-HEAVY SOUP.

MAKES 7 cups

INGREDIENTS

- 1   28-oz. can diced tomatoes with Italian herbs, undrained
- 2   cups water
- 1   14- to 15-oz. can garbanzo beans (chickpeas), rinsed and drained
- 1   cup dried rigatoni or penne pasta
- 1   cup low-sodium vegetable broth or reduced-sodium chicken broth
- 1   cup thinly sliced carrots
- 2   tsp. dried Italian seasoning, crushed
- 2   to 3 cups fresh baby spinach
    Parmesan cheese (optional)

BODY BUILDER

Use cut-up broccoli or chopped red or yellow sweet peppers in place of some of the carrots. Both veggies are loaded with vitamin C, which can help you kick a cold faster.

68

TOOLS

Measuring cups and spoons, can opener, sharp knife, cutting board, large saucepan, wooden spoon

MAKE iT!

1 Put tomatoes, the water, garbanzo beans, pasta, vegetable broth, carrots, and Italian seasoning in the large saucepan. Put saucepan on burner. Turn burner to high heat. Bring to boiling; reduce heat to medium-low heat. Cover and cook about 10 minutes or just until pasta is barely tender, using the wooden spoon to stir every now and then. Turn off burner. Stir in spinach. If you like, top each serving with Parmesan cheese.

PER 1¾ CUPS 213 cal., 2 g fat (0 g sat. fat), 0 mg chol., 725 mg sodium, 40 g carb., 7 g fiber, 11 g sugars, 9 g pro.

DiD YOU KNOW?

Rigatoni got its name because of its shape. (It's an Italian name.) You can use any short, thick pasta in this soup.

STROMBOLI WORLD CUPS

SCORE A GOAL WITH THESE KICKIN'-GOOD PIZZA SPIRALS.

MAKES 6 servings

INGREDIENTS

Nonstick cooking spray

1   13.8-oz. package refrigerated pizza dough

½   cup pizza sauce

½   cup chopped green sweet pepper

3   oz. very thinly sliced cooked turkey breast

3   oz. thinly sliced Canadian bacon

1½   cups shredded Italian-blend cheeses

TOOLS

Measuring cups and spoons, sharp knife, cutting board, muffin pan with twelve 2½-inch cups, rolling pin, ruler, silicone spatula, serrated knife, hot pads, wire rack, table knife

MAKE iT!

1 Turn on oven to 375°F. Generously coat twelve 2½-inch muffin cups with cooking spray. Put pizza dough on a lightly floured surface. Use the rolling pin to roll the dough into a 12×10-inch rectangle. Use the ruler to measure it.

2 Pour pizza sauce on dough rectangle. Spread evenly with silicone spatula. Sprinkle the sweet pepper evenly over the sauce. Lay turkey and Canadian bacon slices on top of sweet pepper. Sprinkle cheese blend over the meats.

3 Starting from a long side, roll up dough in a spiral; pinch the long seam to seal it. Use the serrated knife to slice the spiral into 12 equal pieces. Place a piece, cut side up, in each prepared muffin cup.

4 Carefully put pan in the oven. Bake 15 to 20 minutes or until dough is golden and cheese is melted. Turn off oven. Use hot pads to remove pan from oven. Put pan on a wire rack; cool in muffin cups 5 minutes. Use the table knife to remove stromboli cups from muffin cups. If desired, serve with additional pizza sauce warmed for dipping.

PER SERVING 300 cal., 9 g fat (5 g sat. fat), 37 mg chol., 888 mg sodium, 35 g carb., 2 g fiber, 5 g sugars, 20 g pro.

COOKING CLASS

Hold the muffin pan over the sink when you coat the cups so you don't get cooking spray on the floor. You don't want to lose your footing!

MAKE IT YOUR WAY

TRIATHLON TORTILLAS

MAKES 8 servings

USE YOUR FAVORITE NACHO TOPPINGS AND RACE TO THE FINISH FOR A WINNING MEAL!

START

1

Turn on oven to 350°F. Spread 2½ cups BITE-SIZE TORTILLA CHIPS in a 13x9-inch pan. Put MEAT in a medium bowl.

PICK

2 cups chopped cooked chicken breast

2 cups shredded cooked pork

12 oz. ground beef, browned and drained

2

Add one 15-oz. can BEANS, rinsed and drained, and 1 cup SALSA to meat. Mix well.

PICK

Small red beans

Black beans

Pinto beans

CHEESE CHALLENGE

3

Spoon half of the meat mixture over the chips. Sprinkle with ¾ cup shredded CHEESE.

PICK

Co-Jack

Cheddar

Mexican-style four-cheese blend

5 TOP with 2½ cups more tortilla chips. Top with the rest of the meat mixture and ¾ cup more cheese. Go back to Step 4 and repeat. Skip to Step 6.

PICK

Salsa

Guacamole

Sour cream

Sliced pitted ripe olives

Green onions

6 Use a pancake turner to put nachos on plates. If you wish, add TOPPINGS.

FINISH

4 Put pan in oven. Bake about 10 minutes or until cheese is melted. Use hot pads to carefully remove pan from oven. Put pan on a wire rack.

BUNNY HILL ALFREDO WITH BACON & PEAS

WARM UP AFTER A DAY ON THE SLOPES WITH AN EASY AND CREAMY ONE-PAN PASTA DINNER.

INGREDIENTS

- 4 slices cooked packaged bacon
- 3 cups dried radiatore, rotini, or penne pasta (8 oz.)
- 1 14.5-oz. can reduced-sodium chicken broth
- 1 cup water
- ¼ tsp. garlic powder
- ¼ tsp. salt
- ¼ tsp. black pepper
- 1 cup frozen peas
- ¼ to ⅓ cup heavy cream
- ¼ cup grated Parmesan cheese

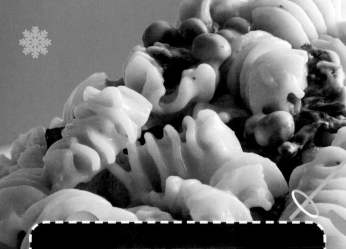

Get a nutrient lift by choosing multigrain pasta for all or half of the pasta. It will give you a natural energy boost.

TOOLS

Measuring cups and spoons, can opener, kitchen scissors, large deep skillet with a lid, wooden spoon

MAKE IT!

1 Using the kitchen scissors, snip bacon into small pieces. Put bacon, pasta, broth, the water, garlic powder, salt, and pepper in the large deep skillet. Put skillet on burner. Turn burner to medium-high heat. Bring to boiling. Turn burner down to medium-low heat. Cover skillet. Simmer 12 to 15 minutes or until pasta is tender but still firm, stirring once with the wooden spoon.

2 Add peas, cream, and cheese to skillet. Stir to combine with the wooden spoon. Cook about 2 minutes more or until heated, stirring constantly. Turn off burner. If you like, snip some more bacon to sprinkle on top.

PER SERVING 363 cal., 11 g fat (6 g sat. fat), 29 mg chol., 641 mg sodium, 49 g carb., 3 g fiber, 4 g sugars, 15 g pro.

PORK & NOODLE SUPER BOWL

GET FUELED UP FOR YOUR END-ZONE CELEBRATION WITH THIS HIGH-SCORING NOODLE BOWL.

MAKES 4 servings

INGREDIENTS

- 12 oz. boneless pork sirloin chops, cut into bite-size strips
- ½ cup low-fat Asian salad dressing
- 4 oz. dry multigrain or whole wheat spaghetti, broken in half
- 1 Tbsp. olive oil
- 6 cups packaged shredded broccoli slaw mix or packaged shredded cabbage with carrot (coleslaw mix)
- ¼ cup toasted sliced almonds or chopped cashews (optional)

MAKE iT!

1 Put pork and ¼ cup of the salad dressing in the medium bowl. Stir to combine. Cover bowl with the plastic wrap and put the bowl in the refrigerator at least 1 hour.

2 Fill the large saucepan three-fourths full with cool water. Put on burner. Turn burner to medium-high heat. When water starts to boil, carefully add the spaghetti to saucepan; stir with the wooden spoon. Cook following package directions until noodles are tender, stirring every now and then. Put colander in sink. Turn off burner. Using the hot pads, carefully pour noodles into colander to drain. Pour the drained noodles back into the pan. Add the remaining ¼ cup salad dressing. Stir to coat noodles.

3 Meanwhile, put olive oil in the extra-large nonstick skillet. Put skillet on burner. Turn burner to medium-high heat. Add the pork; cook and stir with the wooden spoon 3 to 4 minutes or until no pink remains. Turn off burner. Using hot pads, carefully pour pork into pan with the noodles. Put hot skillet back on burner.

4 Put broccoli slaw mix in hot skillet. Turn burner to medium-high heat. Cook and stir with the wooden spoon about 3 minutes or just until broccoli slaw starts to get soft. Turn off burner. Using hot pads, carefully pour broccoli slaw into pan with noodles. Stir to mix. If you wish, sprinkle almonds on each serving.

PER SERVING 317 cal., 9 g fat (2 g sat. fat), 59 mg chol., 360 mg sodium, 34 g carb., 5 g fiber, 10 g sugars, 27 g pro.

DiD YOU KNOW?

You can measure spaghetti using a quarter. Pick up some dried spaghetti and make the bundle as big around as the quarter. That's about 2 ounces. Do that twice and you'll have the right amount for this recipe.

FLY-A-WAFFLE-FRY PIZZA BAKE

LAND A DISC IN THIS CHEESY BASKET TO SCORE A PIZZA-FLAVORED DINNER.

MAKES 6 servings

INGREDIENTS

- 1½ lb. lean ground beef or bulk Italian sausage
- 1½ cups sliced fresh mushrooms
- 1 15-oz. can tomato sauce with Italian seasonings
- ½ of a 2.25-oz. can sliced pitted black olives, drained (optional)
- 1 to 1½ cups shredded mozzarella cheese or shredded Italian-blend cheeses (4 to 6 oz.)
- ⅓ of a 22-oz. package frozen waffle fries

TOOLS

Measuring cups and spoons, can opener, large skillet, wooden spoon, colander, bowl, hot pads, 2-qt. baking dish

MAKE IT!

1 Turn on oven to 400°F. Put the large skillet on burner. Add ground beef and mushrooms to skillet. Turn burner to medium-high heat. Cook about 8 minutes or until beef is cooked through, stirring with the wooden spoon to break up the meat as it cooks. Turn off burner. Put colander in sink over bowl. Using hot pads, carefully pour meat mixture into colander to drain. Return meat to skillet and put on burner. Turn burner to medium heat. Stir in tomato sauce and olives (if using). Heat through. Turn off burner. Spoon meat mixture into the 2-qt. baking dish. Sprinkle with cheese.

COOKING CLASS

When you drain fat from cooked meat, it is important to catch the drippings in a bowl so it doesn't go down the sink. Throw it in the trash when it is cool.

2 Carefully arrange waffle fries in a single layer over hot mixture in dish. Carefully put dish in oven. Bake about 28 minutes or until waffle fries are lightly browned. Turn off oven. Use hot pads to remove dish from oven.

UPSIDE-DOWN PIZZA Instead of using waffle fries, butter one side of eight ½-inch-thick slices French bread. Arrange over hot mixture in dish, buttered sides up. Bake as directed.

PER SERVING 321 cal., 16 g fat (6 g sat. fat), 84 mg chol., 712 mg sodium, 15 g carb., 2 g fiber, 2 g sugars, 29 g pro.

SERVE-AN-ACE MEAT LOAF MUFFINS

ADD SOME SPIN TO YOUR GAME WHEN YOU SERVE THESE VEGGIE-PACKED MINI MEAT LOAVES.

MAKES 6 servings

INGREDIENTS

- 1 egg
- ¼ cup seasoned fine dry bread crumbs
- ¼ cup finely chopped fresh mushrooms
- ¼ cup shredded carrot
- ¼ cup finely chopped onion
- ¼ cup + 2 Tbsp. ketchup
- 2 tsp. reduced-sodium Worcestershire sauce
- ½ tsp. bottled minced garlic
- 1¼ lb. extra-lean ground beef
- 1 Tbsp. honey
- ½ of a 24-oz. package refrigerated sour cream and chive mashed potatoes* (1¼ cups)
- ¼ cup reduced-fat shredded cheddar or Parmesan cheese (1 oz.)

80

TOOLS

Measuring cups and spoons, sharp knife, cutting board, large bowl, fork, muffin pan with twelve 2½-inch cups, small bowl, shallow baking pan, small spoon, instant-read thermometer, hot pads, wire rack, slotted spoon

Turn on the oven to 350°F. Break egg into the large bowl. Lightly beat egg with the fork. Add bread crumbs, mushrooms, carrot, onion, the 2 Tbsp. ketchup, the Worcestershire sauce, and garlic. Stir to mix well. Add ground beef; use your clean hands to mix well. (If you like, use a wooden spoon to mix.)

Use your clean hands to lightly press meat mixture into twelve 2½-inch muffin cups (about ⅓ cup each). Place muffin pan in the shallow baking pan. In the small bowl combine the ¼ cup ketchup and the honey; stir with a small spoon to mix. Spoon mixture evenly over meat loaf muffins.

Carefully put pan in oven. Bake about 30 minutes or until the instant-read thermometer inserted into the centers of the muffins registers 160°F.

Meanwhile, heat potatoes following package directions. Stir cheese into the 1¼ cups potatoes. Use hot pads to remove muffin pan from oven. Put muffin pan on wire rack. Carefully spoon a rounded tablespoon of potatoes on each meat loaf muffin. Use hot pads to put pan back in oven. Bake about 5 minutes more or until cheese is melted. Turn off oven. Use hot pads to remove pan from oven.

Put pan on a wire rack; cool in muffin cups 10 minutes. Use the slotted spoon to scoop muffins out of pan.

Cover remaining mashed potatoes and store in the refrigerator up to 3 days. Use as a side dish with another meal.

280 cal., 11 g fat (5 g sat. fat), 103 mg chol., 543 mg sodium, 20 g carb., 1 g fiber, 8 g sugars, 24 g pro.

Make these muffins ahead or reheat leftovers as directed. Cool baked muffins completely. Place cooled muffins in a single layer in an airtight container; cover. Freeze up to 1 month. Thaw in the refrigerator. Microwave, one at a time, about 1 minute or until heated through.

BASES LOADED SHEET-PAN DINNER

MAKE IT YOUR WAY

MAKES 4 servings

START

CHOOSE YOUR PITCH AND MAKE A GRAND SLAM ONE-PAN SUPPER.

425°

1 Turn on oven to 425°F. Put a piece of foil in a 15x10-inch baking pan to cover bottom. Put MEAT in pan. Use a cooking brush to spread 1 tsp. OLIVE OIL over meat.

Two 8-oz. skinless, boneless chicken breast halves

One 1-lb. pork tenderloin

PICK

PICK

BBQ 1 Tbsp. packed brown sugar, 2 tsp. chili powder, ½ tsp. smoked paprika, ¼ tsp. salt.

SWEET 'N' SPICY 1 Tbsp. packed brown sugar, ½ tsp. pumpkin pie spice, ½ tsp. orange zest, ¼ tsp. salt, ⅛ tsp. cayenne pepper.

2 Pick a RUB and mix it up in a small bowl. Use your clean fingers to evenly spread RUB over meat.

GREEK 2 tsp. dried oregano, 1 tsp. dried basil, ½ tsp. lemon-pepper seasoning, ¼ tsp. garlic powder.

4 Put pan in oven. Roast 25 to 30 minutes or until vegetables are tender when you poke them with a fork and an instant-read thermometer inserted into the center of the pork reads 145°F. (For chicken, roast 20 to 25 minutes or until 165°F.)

PICK

1-inch cubes potatoes

1-inch cubes peeled butternut squash

1-inch pieces sweet peppers

Button mushrooms (halved)

Carrots (sliced)

½-inch wedges onion

Whole cherry tomatoes

165

5 Turn off oven. Use hot pads to remove pan from oven. Put pan on a wire rack. Cover meat with foil. Let stand 3 minutes. Put meat on cutting board and slice with a sharp knife.

3 Put 6 cups VEGETABLES in a large bowl. Add 1 Tbsp. OLIVE OIL, ½ tsp. SALT, and ½ tsp. BLACK PEPPER. Stir to coat. Put in pan around meat.

BBQ sauce

Ranch dressing

PICK

Light vinaigrette dressing

6 Serve meat with vegetables and desired SAUCE.

FINISH

FAST-FUELING SNACKS

STAY UP TO SPEED BETWEEN
MEALS BY CHOOSING ENERGY-
BOOSTING MUNCHIES.

JET PLANE PUDDING POPS

THESE FROZEN GOODIES WILL HAVE YOU ZOOMING ACROSS THE SKY.

MAKES 12 pops

INGREDIENTS

- ¾ cup sugar
- 3 Tbsp. cornstarch
- 3 cups milk
- 1 Tbsp. butter
- 1 Tbsp. vanilla

TOOLS

Measuring cups and spoons, medium saucepan, whisk, hot pads, spoon, 12 freezer pop molds

MAKE IT!

1 Put the sugar and cornstarch in the medium saucepan. Whisk to mix. Add milk. Whisk to mix. Put pan on burner. Turn burner to medium heat. Cook and stir pudding until thickened and bubbly. Cook and stir 2 minutes more. Turn off burner. Using hot pads, remove saucepan from heat. Add butter and vanilla. Stir until butter is melted and stirred in. Cover and let cool 1 hour.

2 Spoon mixture into 12 freezer pop molds. Cover molds. Freeze 6 to 24 hours or until pops are firm.

3 To remove frozen pops from the molds, quickly run warm water over the surface of the molds. Remove pops from molds.

PER POP 98 cal., 2 g fat (1 g sat. fat), 7 mg chol., 37 mg sodium, 17 g carb., 0 g fiber, 16 g sugars, 2 g pro.

CARAMEL PUDDING POPS Make pops as directed, except spoon ½ tsp. caramel ice cream topping onto each pop and wiggle sticks slightly before freezing.

PER POP Same as above, except 108 cal., 192 mg sodium, 20 g carb., 18 g sugars

CHOCOLATE PUDDING POPS Make pops as directed, except stir 4 oz. chopped semisweet chocolate into the thickened pudding until it is melted. Let pudding cool 30 minutes instead of 1 hour in Step 1.

PER POP 143 cal., 5 g fat (3 g sat. fat), 8 mg chol., 37 mg sodium, 23 g carb., 1 g fiber, 20 g sugars, 2 g pro.

LOCOMOTIVE KETTLE CORN

BUILD UP A HEAD OF STEAM WITH A HANDFUL OF THIS CHEWY TREAT.

MAKES 8 cups

INGREDIENTS

¼ cup raisins

¼ cup chopped dried apples

½ tsp. ground cinnamon

¼ tsp. ground ginger

1 3.2-oz. package unpopped microwave kettle popcorn

MAKE IT!

1 Put raisins, apples, cinnamon, and ginger in a bowl. Stir to mix.

2 Pop popcorn in the microwave according to package directions. Carefully open popcorn bag and sprinkle fruit mixture over hot popcorn. Using hot pads, hold bag shut and shake to combine. To serve, pour popcorn mixture into a large bowl.

PER CUP 80 cal., 4 g fat (1 g sat. fat), 0 mg chol., 40 mg sodium, 10 g carb., 1 g fiber, 4 g sugars, 1 g pro.

K.C. EXPRESS

ROCKET SHIP SKEWERS

BLAST OFF TO THE MOON AND BEYOND AFTER EATING THESE PROTEIN-FILLED SNACKS.

MAKES 4 skewers

INGREDIENTS

2 miniature wax-wrapped semisoft light cheese rounds (Babybel)

1 oz. deli-sliced turkey breast

1 oz. deli-sliced ham

4 2-inch-tall triangles watermelon, cantaloupe, or honeydew melon

1 Unwrap cheese rounds. Use a table knife to cut cheese rounds in half. Put a 4-inch frilled pick through the flat side of the cheese. Repeat with three more picks and the remaining cheese. Layer turkey and ham slices on top of each other. Roll up into a spiral. Cut spiral into four pieces. Put spiral pieces on picks next to cheese. Put melon triangles on picks through short sides so the melon point is on top.

PER SKEWER 62 cal., 3 g fat (2 g sat. fat), 17 mg chol., 247 mg sodium, 4 g carb., 0 g fiber, 3 g sugars, 5 g pro.

POSITIVE-CHARGE ENERGY POPPERS

GIVE YOURSELF A POP OF POWER WITH ONE OR TWO OF THESE NO-BAKE BALLS.

MAKES 30 poppers

INGREDIENTS

- 1¼ cups regular rolled oats
- ½ cup unsweetened shredded coconut, toasted
- ½ cup flaxseed meal
- ¼ cup snipped golden raisins, dried blueberries, dried cherries, or dried cranberries
- ¼ cup sunflower kernels
- 1 Tbsp. chia seeds
- ⅔ cup almond butter
- ⅓ cup honey

TOOLS

Measuring cups and spoons, kitchen scissors, 15×10-inch pan, hot pads, wire rack, medium bowl, wooden spoon, small bowl

MAKE IT!

To toast oats, turn on the oven to 350°F. Spread oats in a 15x10-inch baking pan. Put in oven. Bake 5 minutes. Use hot pads to remove pan from oven. Stir oats. Bake 5 to 10 minutes more or until golden. Turn off oven. Use hot pads to remove pan from oven. Place pan on a wire rack. Let oats cool.

Put oats, coconut, flaxseed meal, raisins, sunflower kernels, and chia seeds in the medium bowl. Stir to mix. Put the almond butter and honey in the small bowl. Stir to mix. Add almond butter mixture to cereal mixture. Stir to mix. Use your hands to shape mixture into 1-inch balls.

TO STORE Layer poppers between sheets of waxed paper in an airtight container; put on lid. Store balls in the refrigerator up to 1 week

PER POPPER 96 cal., 6 g fat (2 g sat. fat), 0 mg chol., 21 mg sodium, 9 g carb., 2 g fiber, 5 g sugars, 3 g pro.

BODY BUILDER

This is the perfect snack for when you're playing hard. The oats and almond butter fill you up. The dried fruit and honey give you a big boost of energy.

FLEET-FEET FRUIT SALAD

GET THE QUICK ENERGY YOU NEED TO WIN THE RACE FROM THIS SWEET SALAD.

MAKES 8 servings

INGREDIENTS

- 1 orange
- 2 Tbsp. honey
- 1 cup halved green and/or red seedless grapes
- 1 cup fresh blueberries
- 1 cup halved fresh strawberries
- 1 cup fresh raspberries and/or blackberries
- 2/3 cup chopped apple (1 medium)

TOOLS

Measuring cups and spoons, cutting board, sharp knife, fine grater, citrus juicer, large bowl, silicone spatula

MAKE iT!

1 Use the fine grater to remove 1 tsp. zest from orange. Be careful not to remove any of the white part. Cut orange in half. Use the citrus juicer to juice orange. Measure ¼ cup juice. Put orange zest, orange juice, and honey in the large bowl. Whisk to mix.

2 Add grapes, blueberries, and strawberries to the bowl. Gently stir with the silicone spatula to coat with juice mixture. Cover bowl and put in the refrigerator up to 24 hours.

3 Before serving, add raspberries and apple. Stir gently to mix.

PER SERVING 137 cal., 1 g fat (0 g sat. fat), 0 mg chol., 3 mg sodium, 35 g carb., 5 g fiber, 27 g sugars, 1 g pro.

cooking class

If you don't have a citrus juicer, you can still squeeze out the juice easily. If the orange is cold, microwave it 10 seconds, then roll it on the counter a few times to loosen the fruit from the skin. Cut the orange in half. Poke the cut surface of the orange all over with a fork and squeeze it over a bowl.

BERRY-BLAST SLUSHIES

BLEND UP A HYDRATING FRUIT DRINK TO KEEP YOU AND YOUR FRIENDS PLAYING HARD.

MAKES 6 servings

INGREDIENTS

- 2 cups fresh strawberries and/or raspberries
- 1½ cups ice cubes
- ¼ cup honey
- 2 Tbsp. lemon juice
- 1½ cups berry-flavor sparkling water, chilled

MAKE IT!

1 Put berries, ice cubes, honey, and lemon juice in the blender. Cover and blend until smooth. Stop now and then to scrape sides of blender.

2 Pour mixture evenly into the glasses (a little more than ⅓ cup each). Pour ¼ cup sparkling water into each glass.

PER SERVING 59 cal., 0 g fat, 0 mg chol., 6 mg sodium, 16 g carb., 1 g fiber, 14 g sugars, 0 g pro.

VERY BERRY FLOATS Add a scoop of frozen vanilla yogurt ice cream to each serving.

PER SERVING 179 cal., 3 g fat (2 g sat. fat), 25 mg chol., 81 mg sodium, 33 g carb., 1 g fiber, 31 g sugars, 6 g pro.

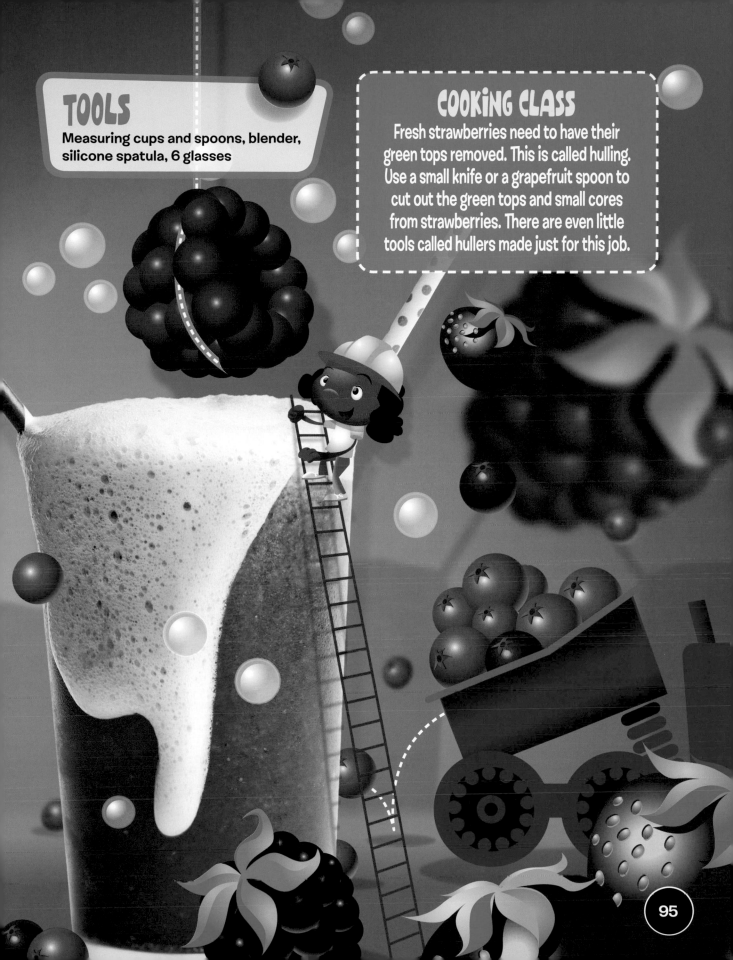

TOOLS

Measuring cups and spoons, blender, silicone spatula, 6 glasses

COOKING CLASS

Fresh strawberries need to have their green tops removed. This is called hulling. Use a small knife or a grapefruit spoon to cut out the green tops and small cores from strawberries. There are even little tools called hullers made just for this job.

GRAND PRIX BANANA BITES

MAKES 4 servings

MAKE A PIT STOP BETWEEN RACES TO GRAB THESE FAST SNACKS.

INGREDIENTS

- ⅓ cup cornflakes or bran cereal flakes, coarsely crushed
- 2 Tbsp. flaked coconut
- 2 Tbsp. vanilla fat-free yogurt
- 2 Tbsp. peanut butter
- 2 small bananas, peeled

DID YOU KNOW?

Rubbing the inside of a banana peel on a mosquito bite can help stop the itch.

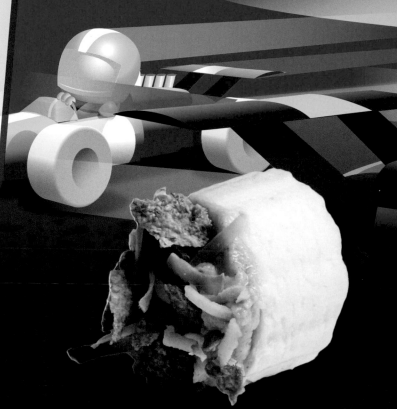

TOOLS

Measuring cups and spoons, cutting board, small skillet, wooden spoon, small bowl, spoon, table knife

MAKE IT!

1 Put cornflakes and coconut in the small skillet. Put pan on burner. Turn burner to medium heat. Cook 2 to 3 minutes or until coconut starts to brown, stirring all the time with the wooden spoon. Turn off burner. Remove pan from burner. Let cool.

2 Put the yogurt and peanut butter in the small bowl. Stir to mix. Cut each banana into eight slices. Spread peanut butter mixture on banana slices. Sprinkle slices with the cornflake mixture; press lightly with your fingers to make it stick.

PER SERVING 110 cal., 5 g fat (1 g sat. fat), 0 mg chol., 62 mg sodium, 16 g carb., 2 g fiber, 8 g sugars, 3 g pro.

For an easy, mess-free way to crush cornflakes, put them in a resealable plastic bag. Press out most of the air and seal bag. Use a rolling pin to crush cornflakes.

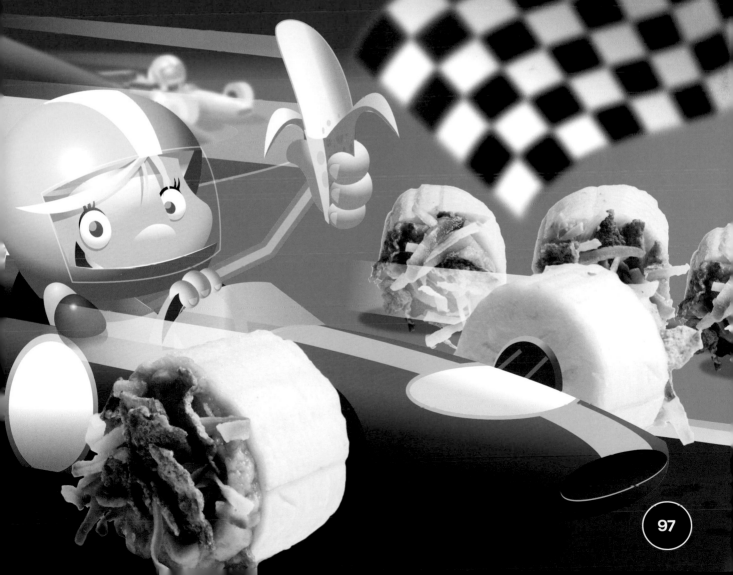

ROLLER COASTER COOKIE DOUGH DIP

DON'T LET THE SECRET INGREDIENT IN THIS CHOCOLATE CHIP DIP THROW YOU FOR A LOOP!

MAKES 18 servings

INGREDIENTS

½	cup water
¼	cup pitted dates
1	15-oz. can no-salt-added cannellini beans, rinsed and drained
½	cup creamy peanut butter
1	tsp. vanilla
⅛	tsp. salt
½	cup dark chocolate chips
¼	cup quick-cooking rolled oats
36	chocolate or honey graham cracker squares

TOOLS

Measuring cups and spoons, small saucepan with lid, can opener, fine-mesh sieve, food processor, silicone spatula, medium bowl

MAKE IT!

1 Put water and dates in the small saucepan. Put pan on burner. Turn burner to high heat. Bring water to boiling. Turn heat down to medium-low. Cover pan with lid. Cook about 5 minutes or until dates are very soft. Turn off burner. Remove pan from heat and let cool.

2 Pour dates and cooking liquid into the food processor. Add beans, peanut butter, vanilla, and salt. Cover and process until smooth, stopping occasionally to scrape the sides of bowl with the spatula.

3 Use the spatula to scoop bean mixture into the medium bowl. (Have an adult help you remove the food processor blade.) Add chocolate chips and oats to bean mixture. Stir to mix.

4 Let dip stand 5 minutes before serving. Break graham cracker squares in half for dipping, or spread dip between whole graham cracker squares to make sandwiches.

TO STORE Put dip in an airtight container; add lid. Store in the refrigerator up to 3 days or freeze up to 6 months.

PER SERVING 161 cal., 7 g fat (2 g sat. fat), 0 mg chol., 143 mg sodium, 22 g carb., 3 g fiber, 8 g sugars, 4 g pro.

COOKING CLASS

Food processors are great tools for making smooth dips. But they have very sharp curved blades that are tricky to use. Have an adult handle the blade for you when you assemble the food processor.

FILL'ER UP GRANOLA CUPS

EAT THESE CUPS TO FUEL UP AND YOU WON'T RUN OUT OF GAS ALL AFTERNOON.

YOGURT

MAKES 12 servings

INGREDIENTS

- 2 cups regular rolled oats
- ½ cup wheat germ
- ¼ cup dry-roasted sunflower kernels
- ¼ cup flaked coconut
- ¼ cup butter
- ¼ cup packed brown sugar
- 2 Tbsp. honey or maple syrup
- ¼ tsp. ground cinnamon
  Nonstick cooking spray
- 1 cup desired-flavor low-fat yogurt
- 1½ cups chopped fresh fruit and/or berries

TOOLS

Measuring cups and spoons, cutting board, sharp knife, large bowl, small saucepan, wooden spoon, hot pads, muffin pan with twelve 2½-inch cups, wire rack, small spoon, table knife

MAKE IT!

1 Put the oats, wheat germ, sunflower kernels, and coconut in the large bowl. Put butter, brown sugar, honey, and cinnamon in the small saucepan. Put pan on burner. Turn burner to medium heat. Cook until sugar is dissolved, stirring all the time with the wooden spoon. Turn off burner. Use hot pads to remove pan from burner.

Carefully pour butter mixture over oat mixture. Stir to mix. Cover and put in the refrigerator until chilled.

2 Turn on oven to 325°F. Lightly coat twelve 2½-inch muffin cups with cooking spray (tip, *page 9*). Using a ¼-cup measuring cup, scoop mixture into prepared muffin cups. Wet your hands with water and press oat mixture onto bottoms and up sides of cups.

3 Bake about 15 minutes or until edges are light brown. Turn off oven. Use hot pads to remove muffin pan from oven. Place pan on a wire rack. If centers puff during baking, press with the back of the small spoon. Let cool. Use the table knife to loosen cups from pan and remove cups.

4 Spoon yogurt into granola cups and top with fruit.

TO MAKE AHEAD Layer the unfilled cooled cups between sheets of waxed paper in an airtight container; add lid. Put in the refrigerator up to 3 days or put in the freezer up to 3 months. Thaw cups if frozen. Fill as directed.

PER SERVING 178 cal., 8 fat (4 g sat. fat), 11 mg chol., 64 mg sodium, 24 g carb., 3 g fiber, 12 g sugars, 5 g pro.

SUPERSONIC SNACK MIX

CRUNCH THROUGH THIS ZESTY SNACK MIX AND BREAK THE SOUND BARRIER.

MAKES 9 cups

INGREDIENTS

- 4 cups crispy corn and rice cereal
- 1 1.75-oz. can shoestring potatoes
- 2 cups crisp breadsticks, broken into 2-inch pieces
- 2 cups bite-size cheese crackers
- 1 6-oz. can (about 1 cup) smoked whole almonds (optional)
- ¼ cup butter, cut up
- 3 Tbsp. Italian vinaigrette salad dressing
- ¼ cup grated Parmesan cheese
- ¼ tsp. garlic powder

TOOLS

Measuring cups and spoons, large roasting pan, small saucepan, wooden spoon, hot pads, wire rack

MAKE IT!

1 Turn on oven to 300°F. Put cereal, shoestring potatoes, breadsticks, cheese crackers, and, if desired, almonds in the large roasting pan.

2 Put butter and salad dressing in the small saucepan. Put saucepan on burner. Turn burner to low heat. Cook until butter is melted. Turn off burner. Add cheese and garlic powder. Use the wooden spoon to mix. Use hot pads to hold saucepan; drizzle butter mixture over cereal mixture. Stir to coat cereal mixture.

3 Carefully put pan in oven. Bake 10 minutes. Use hot pads to remove pan from oven. Stir snack mix. Bake 10 minutes more. Remove pan and stir again. Bake 10 minutes more. Turn off oven. Remove pan from oven and place on the wire rack. Let cool.

TO STORE Put cooled mix in an airtight container; add lid. Store up to 3 days at room temperature.

128 cal., 6 g fat (3 g sat. fat), 10 mg chol., 238 mg sodium, 16 g carb., 1 g fiber, 1 g sugars, 3 g pro.

COOKING CLASS

One stick of butter equals ½ cup or 8 tablespoons. You will need half of a stick for this recipe. Cutting the butter into smaller pieces helps it melt faster.

MAKE IT YOUR WAY

START

KICKIN' KARATE SUSHI ROLLS

MAKES 1 serving

PICK

1 Use a sharp knife to cut crusts off one BREAD slice. Gently roll bread with a rolling pin until very thin.

PICK

Marble rye

Whole wheat

White

2 Top with a thin slice of MEAT.

PICK

Roast beef

Turkey

Ham

3 Top with a thin slice of CHEESE.

Swiss

Mozzarella

Co-Jack

For fun, use a melon baller or small spoon to scoop out most of the center of a 2-inch cucumber piece to make a cup. Fill with DIP: ranch dressing, Thousand Island dressing, or salsa.

ADD A DIP

FiNiSH

4 Use a spreader or table knife to smear SPREAD over cheese.

PiCK

Pesto

Mashed avocado

Cream cheese

5 Put VEGGIES in a strip along one edge of bread. Starting at the edge with veggies, roll up bread. Use a sharp knife to cut roll into three pieces.

Sweet pepper strips

PiCK

Shredded carrot

Pickle spears

Cucumber sticks

Avocado slices

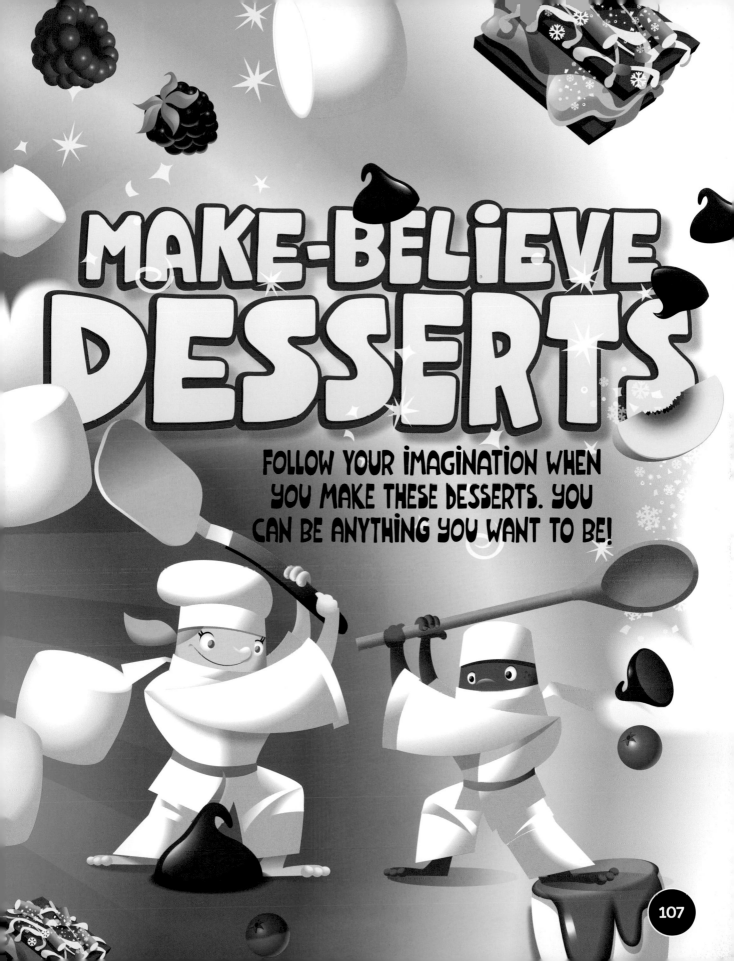

MAKE-BELIEVE DESSERTS

FOLLOW YOUR IMAGINATION WHEN YOU MAKE THESE DESSERTS. YOU CAN BE ANYTHING YOU WANT TO BE!

TREASURE CHEST PEANUT CLUSTERS

DIG INTO THIS TREASURE TROVE OF TASTY TREATS, MATEY!

INGREDIENTS

- 1 cup semisweet chocolate chips
- 6 oz. vanilla-flavor candy coating (almond bark), chopped
- 2 Tbsp. creamy peanut butter
- 1½ cups puffed corn cereal (Kix)
- ½ cup lightly salted dry-roasted peanuts

TOOLS

Measuring cups and spoons, cutting board, sharp knife, tray or large baking sheet, waxed paper, medium heavy saucepan, wooden spoon, 2 small spoons

MAKE IT!

1 Cover the tray or large baking sheet with waxed paper. Put chocolate chips, candy coating, and peanut butter in the medium heavy saucepan. Put pan on burner. Turn burner to medium-low heat. Cook until mixture is melted and smooth, stirring now and then with the wooden spoon. Turn off burner. Remove pan from burner. Add cereal and peanuts. Stir until well coated.

2 Drop cereal mixture by rounded small spoons onto the prepared tray. Put tray in the refrigerator about 15 minutes or until clusters are set (dry to the touch).

TO STORE Layer clusters between sheets of waxed paper in an airtight container; put on lid. Store in the refrigerator up to 1 week or freeze up to 3 months.

PER CLUSTER 105 cal., 7 g fat (4 g sat. fat), 0 mg chol., 22 mg sodium, 11 g carb., 1 g fiber, 9 g sugars, 1 g pro.

COOKING CLASS

Lots of times you will see recipes that tell you to "drop" dough or some mixture onto a baking sheet. To do this, you will need two small spoons (the kind you'd use to eat your cereal, not measuring spoons). Scoop a spoonful of the cereal mixture and use a second spoon to push it off ("drop" it) into a small mound.

ARMY GUY CRISPY BARS

THIS D.R.E. (DESSERT READY TO EAT) WILL KEEP YOUR ARMY IN FIGHTING FORM.

MAKES 16 bars

INGREDIENTS

Butter

3 cups tiny marshmallows

2 Tbsp. butter, softened

3 cups crisp rice cereal

$2/3$ cup tropical blend or regular mixed dried fruit bits, snipped if necessary

$1/2$ cup granola

MAKE IT!

1 Line the 8-inch square baking pan with foil, extending foil over edges. Butter foil.

2 Put marshmallows and the 2 Tbsp. butter in the large bowl. Microwave 1 to 2 minutes or until melted, stirring once. Add the cereal, dried fruit, and granola. Stir to mix.

3 Spoon mixture into the prepared pan. Rub a small amount of butter on a sheet of waxed paper. Use it to press cereal mixture firmly into pan. If you like, sprinkle with additional dried fruit and granola; press lightly. Let stand 1 hour or until set (dry to the touch). Use foil to lift bars out of pan. Cut into bars.

TO STORE Layer bars between pieces of waxed paper in an airtight container; add lid. Store at room temperature up to 3 days.

PER BAR 87 cal., 2 g fat (1 g sat. fat), 4 mg chol., 61 mg sodium, 17 g carb., 1 g fiber, 10 g sugars, 1 g pro.

To line a pan with foil, turn pan upside down. Tear a piece of foil larger than pan and shape over pan bottom. Lift shaped foil off pan. Turn pan over. Fit foil into it. Leave extra foil hanging over edges to act as handles.

HOCUS-POCUS CAKE

A WOODEN SPOON IS YOUR MAGIC WAND FOR TURNING A BANANA SPLIT INTO A CAKE.

MAKES 18 servings

INGREDIENTS

Nonstick cooking spray

1 package 2-layer-size yellow cake mix

1 cup milk

3 eggs

⅓ cup vegetable oil

1 package 4-serving-size banana cream instant pudding and pie filling mix

2 cups milk

1 cup seedless strawberry jam, melted

2 medium bananas, sliced

2 cups sliced strawberries

1 8-oz. container frozen whipped dessert topping, thawed

Toppings: chocolate-flavor ice cream syrup, chopped nuts, maraschino cherries

TOOLS

Measuring cups and spoons, 13×9-inch baking pan, large bowl, electric mixer, silicone spatula, toothpick, hot pads, wire rack, medium bowl, whisk, wooden spoon with round handle, offset spatula

MAKE IT!

1. Turn on oven to 350°F. Lightly coat the 13x9-inch baking pan with cooking spray. Put the cake mix, the 1 cup milk, the eggs, and oil in the large bowl. Beat with the mixer on low speed just until combined. Stop mixer and scrape sides of bowl with the silicone spatula. Beat on medium speed 2 minutes, stopping and scraping bowl now and then. Pour batter into the prepared pan. Use spatula to spread it evenly.

2. Put pan in oven. Bake 20 to 25 minutes or until a toothpick inserted in center comes out clean. Turn off oven. Use hot pads to remove pan and put on wire rack. Cool 5 minutes.

3. While the cake is cooling, put pudding mix in the medium bowl with the 2 cups milk. Beat with the whisk 2 minutes, making sure all lumps are gone.

4. Use the round handle of the wooden spoon to poke holes into cake. Space holes 1 inch apart. Use the offset spatula to spread melted jam over the top of the warm cake. Pour pudding over the jam. Spread pudding over cake. Cool completely.

5. Arrange banana and strawberry slices on top of cake. Spoon whipped topping over cake. Use the clean offset spatula to spread evenly. Serve cake with desired toppings. Cover and store leftovers in the refrigerator up to 24 hours.

PER SERVING 325 cal., 12 g fat (4 g sat. fat), 35 mg chol., 305 mg sodium, 49 g carb., 1 g fiber, 22 g sugars, 5 g pro.

DID YOU KNOW?

This kind of cake is called a poke cake. It's important to use a wooden spoon with a round handle. That is what you use to poke the holes. If you don't have one like that, use a skewer.

CHOCOLATE NINJA FONDUE

SILENTLY SPEAR YOUR FAVORITE FRUIT PIECES AND CLOAK THEM IN A DARK CHOCOLATE DISGUISE.

MAKES 16 servings

INGREDIENTS

- 1 8-oz. container frozen light whipped dessert topping, thawed
- 1 10- or 12-oz. package dark chocolate chips
- 1/4 cup milk

  Assorted fruit, such as strawberries, raspberries, pineapple chunks, apple slices, halved kiwifruit slices, and/or peach chunks

  Milk (optional)

TOOLS

Measuring cups, 1½- or 2-qt. slow cooker, wooden spoon, whisk, sixteen 6-inch wooden skewers

MAKE IT!

1 Put whipped topping and chocolate chips in the 1½- or 2-qt. slow cooker. Cover and cook on low setting 30 to 45 minutes or until chocolate is melted. Stir once or twice during cooking (whipped topping will deflate). Add the ¼ cup milk, 1 tablespoon at a time, stirring with the whisk until it is thick but still pourable.

2 Meanwhile, for fruit kabobs, thread assorted fruit onto sixteen 6-inch wooden skewers.

3 Keep fondue warm on warm or low setting. Of, if desired, spoon it into a bowl. Dip fruit kabobs in fondue or spoon it over the kabobs. If fondue becomes too thick, stir in a little additional milk.

PER SERVING 159 cal., 7 g fat (5 g sat. fat), 1 mg chol., 4 mg sodium, 21 g carb., 3 g fiber, 15 g sugars, 1 g pro.

COOKING CLASS

Don't have a 1½- or 2-qt. slow cooker? Use a medium saucepan. Put pan on burner. Turn burner to low heat. Cook until chocolate is melted, stirring now and then. Add milk as directed in Step 1. Turn off burner and spoon fondue into a bowl to serve.

GOIN' BANANAS ICE CREAM

PROCESS FROZEN FRUIT FOR A DAIRY-FREE "ICE CREAM" TREAT.

MAKES 3 cups

INGREDIENTS

- 4 medium bananas, peeled, sliced, and frozen
- ¼ cup refrigerated unsweetened coconut milk
- 2 tsp. vanilla

MAKE IT!

1 Put all ingredients in a food processor (see "Cooking Class," *page 99*). (Use the bananas right from the freezer; don't let them thaw.) Cover and process until smooth. Serve immediately for soft-serve ice cream. Or spoon ice cream into an airtight container; add lid. Put in the freezer at least 4 hours for scoopable ice cream. Store in freezer up to 1 week.

CHOCOLATE ICE CREAM Make as directed, except add 2 Tbsp. unsweetened cocoa powder and go down to 2 Tbsp. coconut milk.

PER ½ CUP PLAIN AND CHOCOLATE 76 cal., 0 g fat, 0 mg chol., 3 mg sodium, 18 g carb., 2 g fiber, 10 g sugars, 1 g pro.

STRAWBERRY-RASPBERRY ICE CREAM Make as directed, except add ½ cup strawberries and ½ cup raspberries and go down to 2 Tbsp. coconut milk. Makes 4 cups.

PER ½ CUP Same as above, except 63 cal., 1 mg sodium, 15 g carb., 8 g sugars

PEANUT BUTTER ICE CREAM Make as directed, except add ¼ cup peanut butter or almond butter and go down to 2 Tbsp. coconut milk.

PER ½ CUP 139 cal., 6 g fat (1 g sat. fat), 0 mg chol., 47 mg sodium, 21 g carb., 3 g fiber, 11 g sugars, 3 g pro.

CLOWNIN'-AROUND FRUIT PIZZA

THE FRUIT MAKES A BIG TOP OF FLAVORS AND COLORS ON THIS FROZEN DESSERT.

MAKES 12 servings

INGREDIENTS

- 1 recipe Goin' Bananas Ice Cream (*opposite*)
- 2 cups crisp rice cereal
- 1 Tbsp. unsweetened cocoa powder
- 2 Tbsp. coconut oil or butter, melted
- 2 Tbsp. honey

Toppers, such as blackberries, raspberries, sliced peaches, sliced bananas, halved grapes, and/or mandarin orange slices

MAKE IT!

1 Prepare Goin' Bananas Ice Cream. Put it in the freezer until needed.

2 For crust, cover a 12-inch pizza pan with parchment paper. Put cereal and cocoa powder in a medium bowl. Stir to mix. Add oil and honey. Stir to mix. Pour onto the prepared pan and spread into a 10-inch circle. Put pan in freezer 5 to 10 minutes or until crust is firm.

3 If necessary, let ice cream stand at room temperature just until soft enough to spread. Spoon ice cream onto crust. Use a silicone spatula to spread ice cream over crust, but leave a 1-inch border around edge. Add toppers. Put pizza in freezer 20 to 30 minutes or until ice cream is nearly firm.

4 Use a pizza cutter to cut pizza into wedges. Put any leftover wedges into an airtight container; add lid. Store in freezer.

PER SERVING 111 cal., 4 g fat (2 g sat. fat), 0 mg chol., 27 mg sodium, 17 g carb., 2 g fiber, 9 g sugars, 2 g pro.

ROUND 'EM UP COOKIES

WRANGLE UP SOME FRIENDS FOR A COOKIE STAMPEDE.

MAKES 24 cookies

INGREDIENTS

- ¼ cup butter
- ¼ cup shortening
- ¼ cup packed brown sugar
- ½ tsp. baking soda
- ½ tsp. salt
- 1 egg
- 1½ tsp. vanilla
- 1 cup all-purpose flour
- ½ cup dark or semisweet chocolate chips

DID YOU KNOW?

If you add 1 Tbsp. honey to this recipe with the egg in Step 2, the cookies will be a little sweeter and soft like cake.

TOOLS

Measuring cups and spoons, medium bowl, electric mixer, silicone spatula, wooden spoon, 2 small spoons or small cookie scoop, 2 cookie sheets, hot pads, pancake turner, wire rack

MAKE iT!

1 Turn on oven to 375°F. Put butter and shortening in the medium bowl. Beat with the mixer on medium to high speed 30 seconds. Add brown sugar, baking soda, and salt. Beat on medium speed 2 minutes, stopping the mixer a few times to scrape the bowl with the silicone spatula.

2 Add egg and vanilla. Beat on medium speed until combined. Add flour. Beat on low speed until combined. Use the wooden spoon to stir in chocolate chips.

3 Drop dough by small spoons (see "Cooking Class," *page 109*) or a small cookie scoop onto ungreased cookie sheets. Leave 2 inches between dough mounds.

4 Put cookie sheets in oven. Bake 6 to 8 minutes or just until edges of cookies are light brown. Turn off oven. Use hot pads to remove cookie sheets from oven. Cool on cookie sheets 2 minutes. Use the pancake turner to transfer cookies to the wire rack. Let cool.

TO STORE Put cookies between sheets of waxed paper in an airtight container; add lid. Store at room temperature up to 1 day, chill up to 3 days, or freeze up to 1 month.

PER COOKiE 91 cal., 6 g fat (3 g sat. fat), 13 mg chol., 95 mg sodium, 9 g carb., 0 g fiber, 5 g sugars, 1 g pro.

SNOW FAIRY ICE CREAM SANDWICHES

THESE FROZEN GOODIES ARE SPARKLY GOOD.

MAKES 8 sandwiches

INGREDIENTS

- 16 chocolate graham cracker squares
- ¼ cup salted pretzels, coarsely chopped
- 4 toffee candies, crushed
- 3 oz. semisweet chocolate chips or white chocolate chips
- ½ tsp. vegetable oil
  Colored sugar (optional)
- 1 cup light strawberry ice cream or frozen yogurt, slightly softened

TOOLS

Measuring cups and spoons, large baking pan, waxed paper, 2 small bowls, silicone spatula, small resealable freezer bag, scissors, spoon, plastic wrap

MAKE iT!

1 Cover the large baking pan with waxed paper. Place eight of the graham cracker squares on the waxed paper. Put the pretzels and toffee candies in one of the small bowls.

2 Put chocolate and oil in the other small bowl. Microwave 15 to 30 seconds or just until chocolate is melted. Stir until smooth. Use the silicone spatula to scrape melted chocolate into the freezer bag. Seal bag. Use scissors to snip off a very small corner of the bag. Squeezing bag, gently drizzle chocolate over graham crackers on the baking pan. Sprinkle pretzel and toffee mixture on graham crackers while chocolate is wet. If desired, sprinkle with colored sugar. Put baking sheet in freezer 10 minutes.

3 Spoon 2 Tbsp. of the ice cream onto one of the remaining graham cracker squares. Spread the ice cream and top it with a chocolate-drizzled graham cracker square. Put sandwiches on the baking pan. Repeat with remaining ice cream and graham crackers.

4 Freeze sandwiches 1 hour. Wrap each sandwich with plastic wrap. Store in freezer.

PER SANDWICH 182 cal., 8 g fat (4 g sat. fat), 9 mg chol., 113 mg sodium, 27 g carb., 1 g fiber, 17 g sugars, 2 g pro.

ICEBERG BARK

BRRRRRRR. PICK UP AND EAT THIS FROSTY YOGURT TREAT WITH YOUR FINGERS.

MAKES 24 servings

INGREDIENTS

6 5.3-oz. cartons vanilla bean whole-milk Greek yogurt

2 Tbsp. honey

1 cup fillings, such as semisweet chocolate chips and/or peanuts, almonds, or pistachios

2 cups toppers, such as toasted raw chip coconut, raspberries, blueberries, sunflower seed kernels, and/or cacao nibs

TOOLS

Measuring cups and spoons, 2 large baking sheets or trays, parchment paper, large bowl, silicone spatula

DID YOU KNOW?

Bark candy is the name for candy coating or chocolate that is melted and filled with nuts or other toppings. Break it into pieces to eat.

MAKE IT!

1 Cover two large baking sheets or trays with parchment paper. Put yogurt and honey in the large bowl. Stir to mix with the silicone spatula. Add fillings. Stir to mix.

2 Pour half of the yogurt mixture onto one of the baking sheets and half onto the other. Spread into rectangles. Sprinkle with toppers.

3 Put baking sheets in freezer 2 to 4 hours or until bark is firm. Break bark into 24 irregular pieces. Put bark in an airtight container; add lid. Store bark in freezer.

PER SERVING 133 cal., 9 g fat (4 g sat. fat), 9 mg chol., 52 mg sodium, 11 g carb., 2 g fiber, 8 g sugars, 3 g pro.

KISS-A-FROG COOKIES

IF YOU'RE HOPPING FOR A KISS, YOU'RE ON THE RIGHT PAD.

MAKES 24 cookies

INGREDIENTS

- 1 cup creamy peanut butter
- 1 egg
- ½ cup sugar
- 1 tsp. baking powder
- ½ tsp. vanilla
- ¼ tsp. salt
- ¼ cup sugar
- 24 dark chocolate candy kisses, unwrapped

MAKE IT!

1 Turn on oven to 350°F. Cover a cookie sheet with parchment paper. Put the peanut butter and egg in the medium bowl. Add the ½ cup sugar, the baking powder, vanilla, and salt. Stir to mix. Put the ¼ cup sugar in a shallow dish.

2 On another piece of parchment paper, pat dough into a rectangle. Use the table knife to cut it lengthwise into four rows and crosswise into six rows to make 24 pieces. Roll pieces into balls. Roll balls in the ¼ cup sugar. Place balls 2 inches apart on the prepared cookie sheet. Use the fork to flatten balls until ½ inch thick, making crisscross marks.

3 Put cookie sheet in oven. Bake 10 to 13 minutes or just until centers are set. Turn off oven. Using hot pads, take sheet out of oven. Carefully press a chocolate kiss into each hot cookie's center. Cool on cookie sheet 3 minutes. Use the pancake turner to transfer cookies to the wire rack. Let cool.

TO STORE Put cookies in a single layer in an airtight container; add lid. Store at room temperature up to 3 days or freeze up to 1 month.

PER COOKIE 114 cal., 7 g fat (2 g sat. fat), 9 mg chol., 12 mg sodium, 97 g carb., 1 g fiber, 10 g sugars, 3 g pro.

DID YOU KNOW?

These cookies don't have flour in them like regular cookies. They hold up just fine without it and they're gluten free!

iNDEX

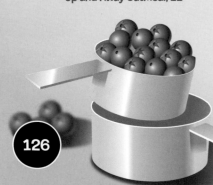

METRIC INFORMATION

PRODUCT DIFFERENCES

Most of the ingredients called for in the recipes in this book are available in most countries. However, some are known by different names. Here are some common American ingredients and their possible counterparts:

- Sugar (white) is granulated, fine granulated, or castor sugar.

- Powdered sugar is icing sugar.

- All-purpose flour is enriched, bleached or unbleached white household flour. When self-rising flour is used in place of all-purpose flour in a recipe that calls for leavening, omit the leavening agent (baking soda or baking powder) and salt.

- Light-color corn syrup is golden syrup.

- Cornstarch is cornflour.

- Baking soda is bicarbonate of soda.

- Vanilla or vanilla extract is vanilla essence.

- Green, red, or yellow sweet peppers are capsicums or bell peppers.

- Golden raisins are sultanas.

- Shortening is solid vegetable oil (substitute Copha or lard).

MEASUREMENT ABBREVIATIONS

MEASUREMENT	ABBREVIATIONS
fluid ounce	fl. oz.
gallon	gal.
gram	g
liter	L
milliliter	ml
ounce	oz.
package	pkg.
pint	pt.

COMMON WEIGHT EQUIVALENTS

IMPERIAL / U.S.	METRIC
½ ounce	14.18 g
1 ounce	28.35 g
4 ounces (¼ pound)	113.4 g
8 ounces (½ pound)	226.8 g
16 ounces (1 pound)	453.6 g
1¼ pounds	567 g
1½ pounds	680.4 g
2 pounds	907.2 g

OVEN TEMPERATURE EQUIVALENTS

FAHRENHEIT SETTING	CELSIUS SETTING
300°F	150°C
325°F	160°C
350°F	180°C
375°F	190°C
400°F	200°C
425°F	220°C
450°F	230°C
475°F	240°C
500°F	260°C
Broil	Broil

*For convection or forced air ovens (gas or electric), lower the temperature setting 25°F/10°C when cooking at all heat levels.

APPROXIMATE STANDARD METRIC EQUIVALENTS

MEASUREMENT	OUNCES	METRIC
⅛ tsp.		0.5 ml
¼ tsp.		1 ml
½ tsp.		2.5 ml
1 tsp.		5 ml
1 Tbsp.		15 ml
2 Tbsp.	1 fl. oz.	30 ml
¼ cup	2 fl. oz.	60 ml
⅓ cup	3 fl. oz.	80 ml
½ cup	4 fl. oz.	120 ml
⅔ cup	5 fl. oz.	160 ml
¾ cup	6 fl. oz.	180 ml
1 cup	8 fl. oz.	240 ml
2 cups	16 fl. oz. (1 pt.)	480 ml
1 qt.	64 fl. oz. (2 pt.)	0.95 L

CONVERTING TO METRIC

centimeters to inches	divide centimeters by 2.54
cups to liters	multiply cups by 0.236
cups to milliliters	multiply cups by 236.59
gallon to liters	multiply gallon by 3.785
grams to ounces	divide grams by 28.35
inches to centimeters	multiply inches by 2.54
kilograms to pounds	divide kilograms by 0.454
liters to cups	divide liters by 0.236
liters to gallons	divide liters by 3.785
liters to pints	divide liters by 0.473
liters to quarts	divide liters by 0.946
milliliters to cups	divide milliliters by 236.59
milliliters to fluid ounces	divide milliliters by 29.57
milliliters to tablespoons	divide milliliters by 14.79
milliliters to teaspoons	divide milliliters by 4.93
ounces to grams	multiply ounces by 28.35
ounces to milliliters	multiply ounces by 29.57
pints to liters	multiply pints by 0.473
pounds to kilograms	multiply pounds by 0.454
quarts to liters	multiply quarts by 0.946
tablespoons to milliliters	multiply tablespoons by 14.79
teaspoons to milliliters	multiply teaspoons by 4.93